D0491426

Grammar for GCSE
English

Series editors: Mike Gould and Paul Higgins

Authors: Mike Gould and Beth Kemp

William Collins' dream of knowledge for all began with the publication of his first book in 1819. A self-educated mill worker, he not only enriched millions of lives, but also founded a flourishing publishing house. Today, staying true to this spirit, Collins books are packed with inspiration, innovation and practical expertise. They place you at the centre of a world of possibility and give you exactly what you need to explore it.

Collins. Freedom to teach.

Published by Collins
An imprint of HarperCollins*Publishers*
The News Building
1 London Bridge Street
London
SE1 9GF

Browse the complete Collins catalogue at
www.collins.co.uk

© HarperCollins Publishers Limited 2013

10 9 8 7 6 5 4 3 2
ISBN 978-0-00-754755-5

Mike Gould and Beth Kemp assert their moral rights to be identified as the authors of this work.

British Library Cataloguing in Publication Data
A Catalogue record for this publication is available from the British Library.

Commissioned by Catherine Martin
Project managed by Alicia Higgins
Edited by Sonya Newland
Proofread by Hugh Hillyard-Parker
Designed by Joerg Hartmannsgruber
Typeset by Jouve India Limited
Cover design by Angela English

With thanks to Jackie Newman and Judy Barratt.

 Packaged by White-Thomson Publishing Ltd.

Acknowledgements

The publishers gratefully acknowledge the permissions granted to reproduce copyright material in this book. While every effort has been made to trace and contact copyright holders, where this has not been possible the publishers will be pleased to make the necessary arrangements at the first opportunity.

Extract from *Of Mice and Men* by John Steinbeck, © 1937 renewed © 1965 by John Steinbeck. Used by permission of Penguin Books Ltd and Viking Penguin, a division of Penguin Group (USA) LLC (p 17); short extract from www.history.co.uk about Leni Riefenstahl. Reprinted with kind permission (p 30); 'Diamonds are forever, but gang stole 32m in three minutes' by Peter Popham, *The Independent*, 19 February, 2013.

Reprinted with permission (p 33); from 'Fracking: the pros and cons', Lord Deben and Emma Hughes (www.countrylife.co.uk/countryside/article/530828/Fracking-the-pros-and-cons.html) Reprinted with permission of *Country Life*/IPC (p 54); screenshot from www.railwaychildren.org.uk reprinted with kind permission (p 58); from *The Good, the Bad and the Multiplex* by Mark Kermode, Random House 2011. Reprinted with permission of The Random House Group Ltd (p 61); from 'Making my skin crawl: tattoos scream for attention' by Tony Parsons, *The Daily Mirror*, 23 June, 2012. Reprinted with permission of *The Daily Mirror* (p 68); from 'Teenagers spend two hours a day social networking while on holiday' by Olivia Goldhill, *The Daily Telegraph*, 12 August, 2013. Reprinted with permission (p 70); 'Anger Lay By Me' by Elizabeth Daryush, from *Selected Poems*, published by Carcanet Press Ltd. Reprinted with permission (p 76); from 'The British summer would be far more tolerable without sunshine' by David Mitchell, *The Observer*, 14 July 2013. Reprinted with permission of Guardian News & Media Ltd © Guardian News & Media Ltd 2013 (p 78); extract from 'Marco Polo Didn't Go There' by Rolf Potts, from *Best of Lonely Planet Travel Guide Writing*/Tony Wheeler, 1st edition, 2009, © 2009 Lonely Planet. Reproduced with permission of Lonely Planet (p 84).

The publishers would like to thank the following for permission to reproduce pictures in these pages:

Cover image ©Alta Oosthuizen/Shutterstock

(t = top, b = bottom)

p 5 Connel/Shutterstock, p 6 Lebrecht Music & Arts/Corbis, p 9 Rashworth/Shutterstock, p 10 Viorel Sima/Shutterstock, p 12 Dmitry Kalinovsky/Shutterstock, p 13 Lance Bellers/Shutterstock, p 14 Vladru/Shutterstock, p 15 John Brown/Alamy, p 16 Zurijeta/Shutterstock, p 17t Iculig/Shutterstock, p 17b Moviestore collection Ltd/Alamy, p 18 Ajfi/Shutterstock, p 20 CREATISTA/Shutterstock, p21 Vitalii Nesterchuk/Shutterstock, p 22 Monkey Business Images/Shutterstock, p 23 Humannet/Shutterstock, p 24 studioVin/Shutterstock, p 25 Stephen Orsillo/Shutterstock, p 27 Stephen Barnes/Scotland/Alamy, p 28 Nenetus/Shutterstock, p 30t Bevan Goldswain/Shutterstock, p 30b AF Archive/Alamy, p 31 Coronado/Shutterstock, p 32 Stephen Coburn/Shutterstock, p 33 Rtimages/Shutterstock, p 34 John Roman Images/Shutterstock, p 35 The Power of Forever Photography/Getty Images, p 36 Andrey Burmakin/Shutterstock, p 37 Ron Ellis/Shutterstock, p 39 Jeff Gilbert/Alamy, p 40t hin255/Shutterstock, p 40b Andrew Burgess/Shutterstock, p 41 Gallinago_media/Shutterstock, p 42 Lewis Phillips/Getty Images, p 43 The Asahi Shimbun/Getty Images, p 45 Spirit of America/Shutterstock, p 46 Kairos69/Shutterstock, p 47 Eric Isselee/Shutterstock, p 48 Nata Sdobnikova/Shutterstock, p 50 Chubykin Arkady/Shutterstock, p 52 Greenshoots Communications/Alamy, p 53 Jesus Keller/Shutterstock, p 54 B Christophe/Alamy, p 55 bikeriderlondon/shutterstock, p 56 Eric Limon/Shutterstock, p 57 Laboko/Shutterstock, p 60 Fotofermer/Shutterstock, p 62 Richard Saker/Rex Features, p 63 Anton Gvozdikov, p 64 MAT/Shutterstock, p 67 Chris Alcock/Shutterstock, p 68 epa european pressphoto agency b.v./Alamy, p 69 Getty Images, p 70 Sean van Tonder/Shutterstock, p 73 The Granger Collection/Topfoto, p 74 Classic Image/Alamy, p 76 Prixel Creative/Shutterstock, p 78 wavebreakmedia/Shutterstock, p 81 blickwinkel/Alamy, p 82t Lisa S./Shutterstock, p 82b adrian arbib/Alamy, p 84 blickwinkel/Alamy, p 87 imagebroker/Alamy, p 88 De Visu/Shutterstock, p 89 koosen/Shutterstock, p 90 Pablo77/Shutterstock, p 91 MaxFX/Shutterstock, p 92 Florin Stana/Shutterstock, p 93 Martin Harvey/Alamy, p 94 Benoit Daoust/Shutterstock, p 95 Ljupco Smokovsk/Shutterstock, p 96 imagebroker/Alamy, p 97 KUCO/Shutterstock, p 98 Rehan Qureshi/Shutterstock, p 99 monticello/Shutterstock, p 100 Sean Nel/Shutterstock, p 102 katalinks/Shutterstock, p 105t Tom Gardner/Alamy, p 105b Dirk Ercken/Shutterstock, p 106t Hulton-Deutsch Collection/Corbis, p 106b Pressmaster/Shutterstock, p 108 Kikovic/Shutterstock, p 109 xuanhuongho/Shutterstock, p 111 lafoto/Shutterstock, p 112 Photobank.ch/Shutterstock, p 113 Accent Alaska.com/Alamy, p 114 leungchopan/Shutterstock, p 116 bikeriderlondon/Shutterstock.

Contents

Chapter 1

The basics

What's it all about?

In order to analyse and use language creatively in your GCSE work, it is important to understand the basics of word classes and punctuation, as well as the fundamentals of sentence structure such as phrases and clauses.

This chapter will show you how to

- understand vocabulary
- understand clauses and phrases
- understand sentence structures
- use punctuation accurately
- use paragraphs effectively.

Understand vocabulary

It will help your GCSE reading and writing to understand the fundamental building blocks of language: word classes.

Getting you thinking

Read this line from the nonsense poem 'Jabberwocky' by Lewis Carroll.

> 'Twas brillig, and the slithy toves did gyre and gimble in the wabe.

1 For each highlighted word, find three real words that could go in that slot.

Exploring the skills

There are eight word classes: nouns, verbs, adjectives, adverbs, pronouns, prepositions, conjunctions and determiners. Each class performs different jobs in a sentence.

In the line above, each of the nonsense words clearly belongs to a certain word class (noun, verb or adjective). You can only replace them with words of the same class.

Nouns

There are two types of noun: common and proper.

	Common nouns	**Proper nouns**
Physical objects or 'things'	table, car, computer, bread	Mercedes, Apple Macintosh
Abstract concepts, emotions, ideas or ideals	peace, religion, anger	Judaism
Living creatures	cat, postman, doctor	Sooty, John, Dr Jones
Places	beach, town	England, Munich

2 Look at the right-hand column in the table. How can you tell if something is a proper noun?

3 Which nonsense words in the line of poetry can you replace with nouns?

- Some nouns have a plural form, ending in 's': *tables, cats, beaches*.

- Nouns can be replaced by a *pronoun*.

John was in the middle of explaining ———— proper noun
when he suddenly raced out of the room. ———— pronoun

Verbs

There are three different types of verb.

- *Main verbs* express an action, process or state: I think, we are going, they would have loved it.

- *Auxiliary verbs* help create the tense: we are leaving, they have eaten it all.

- *Modal verbs* (a type of auxiliary verb) tell us how definite, likely or possible something is: I must do that now, we could say that.

Verbs are **conjugated** to make them agree with a *subject* (the noun or pronoun that is 'doing' the verb):

first person ———————————————— third person
I walk, he walks
first person ———————————————— third person plural
I am, she is, they are
———————————————— third person

Verbs are also conjugated to make different *tenses*:

———————————————— present tense
I walk, I walked
———————————————— past tense
———————————————— present tense
I am, I was
———————————————— past tense

The table below shows how the main tenses in English are formed for **regular verbs**, such as 'to walk' and 'to jump'.

> **Top tip**
>
> Main verbs are essential – every full sentence must have at least one.
>
> Auxiliary verbs, including modals, are used with a main verb.

> **Glossary**
>
> **conjugated:** when verbs change form, usually taking on a different ending
>
> **regular verb:** a verb that follows predictable patterns in forming tenses and agreeing with subjects

Tense	Example	Explanation
Simple present	I jump, he jumps	The ending of the main verb changes according to the tense and subject.
Simple past	I jumped, she jumped	
Present progressive	I am jumping, he is jumping	These tenses are created with an auxiliary verb and a *present participle* of the main verb (ending in '-ing').
Past progressive	I was jumping, she was jumping	
Present perfect	I have jumped, he has jumped	These tenses are created with an auxiliary verb and a *past participle* of the main verb (ending in '-ed').
Past perfect	I had jumped, she had jumped	

Many **irregular verbs** do not follow this pattern exactly. The table below shows some common irregular verbs.

	to be	to eat	to run	to think	to take	to go
Simple present	am, are, is	eat, eats	run, runs	think, thinks	take, takes	go, goes
Simple past	was, were	ate	ran	thought	took	went
Progressive form	was being	was eating	was running	was thinking	was taking	was going
Perfect form	had been	had eaten	had run	had thought	had taken	had gone

1. Which of the nonsense words in Activity 1 seem to be verbs? What tense are they in?

Glossary

irregular verb: a verb that does not follow the standard patterns

Adjectives and adverbs

Adjectives and adverbs are both used to modify (add information to) other words.

Adjectives can describe or modify a noun:

the timid mouse

the tiger was dangerous

Adverbs can modify or intensify a verb or adjective:

I really hope she's ready

she was incredibly busy

2. How many adjectives and adverbs can you think of in two minutes to fit these sentences?

a) The _____ man/house/car.

b) That film/book/game was _____.

c) I am _____ tired.

Developing the skills

Pronouns, prepositions and determiners

Using pronouns, determiners and prepositions can make your writing clear, accurate and effective.

Pronouns and *possessive pronouns* replace a noun, to avoid repetition. You should use them only when it is clear exactly what you are talking about:

I gave it to him

That bike is mine

Prepositions show a relationship between things, usually in space or time: before, on, to, at.

Determiners are added to a noun to make them more specific: a film; this cup; my dog.

6 Which of the words in red are pronouns and which are determiners?

   a) Each child has one drawer.

   b) I want some!

   c) Take one at bedtime.

   d) Leave him alone!

   e) That toy is his.

7 What are the different effects of the highlighted words in the following pairs of sentences?

   a) This is the book for you if you enjoy adventure stories.

      This is a book for you if you enjoy adventure stories.

   b) The sound of gulls calling echoed around the beach, as the large birds swooped over people's heads.

      The sound of gulls calling echoed across the beach, as the large birds swooped towards people's heads.

Applying the skills

In all writing, it is important to choose your words with precision, considering their purpose and effects.

Compare the following sentences:

> The scruffy dog ran across the park towards the man.
>
> The scruffy terrier pelted across the grass towards its owner.

8 Look at the changed words in the second version.

   a) Which are nouns and which are verbs?

   b) What is the effect of the changes?

9 Look at the sentences below and replace the highlighted adjectives and adverbs with more precise alternatives. How many different meanings can you create by changing just one word in each extract?

   a) It is important that we act now to stop this.

   b) The old tree stood out on the hilltop.

   c) Help us to save the poor children.

   d) She walked quickly into the room.

   e) The writer clearly shows the difference between rich and poor.

Check your progress:

Sound progress 》》

I can recognise nouns, verbs, adjectives and adverbs and understand how each one works.

Excellent progress 》》》

I can recognise all the word classes and understand their different functions.

Understand clauses and phrases

You will learn how to
- use clauses of different types accurately and effectively
- use noun phrases and verb phrases to develop variety in sentences.

Understanding how to construct and use clauses and phrases will help you to write varied sentences. This will give your writing flexibility, clarity and precision.

Getting you thinking

A *clause* is the main part of a sentence. It is built around a *verb* and contains a *subject*.

Look at the three clauses in the sentence below.

> Although I had often wondered,
>
> I never did ask Susan
>
> why she hit him.

Although I had often wondered...

1 Identify the main verbs, the auxiliary verbs and the tenses in these clauses.

Exploring the skills

Clauses can be either *main* or *subordinate*.

Main clauses

A main clause must contain a subject and a verb, and it must express a complete thought – it should be able to stand alone as a sentence.

In a main clause, the *subject* carries out the main action and is usually the topic of the clause. The *verb* is the action, state or process in the clause.

She ran as fast as she could. — subject
— verb of action

She thought about it all day. — verb of process
— subject

Sentences are categorised according to the clauses they contain. Main clauses can make up either simple or compound sentences.

Sentence type	Clauses	Clause 1	Clause 2
Simple sentence	One main clause	I saw a really tall man.	
Compound sentence	Two or more main clauses with a coordinating conjunction	I saw a really tall man	and he was wearing a funny hat.
Compound sentence	Two main clauses with a semicolon	I saw a really tall man;	he must have been six-and-a-half feet.

Subordinate clauses

A subordinate clause (sometimes called a dependent clause) does not make sense on its own – it works in the same way as a noun, adjective or adverb within a sentence. It is *added* to a main clause to make a complex sentence.

Sentence type	Clauses	Clause 1	Clause 2
Complex sentence	One main clause + one or more subordinate clauses with a subordinating conjunction	While I was out walking,	I saw a really tall man.
Complex sentence	One main clause + a relative clause	I saw a really tall man,	who was wearing a funny hat.
Complex sentence	One main clause + a non-finite clause	Walking in the park today,	I saw a really tall man.

2 In the two tables, the same ideas are repeated in the examples, but they are expressed in different ways using different types of sentence.

Following the same pattern, produce a series of five sentences built around this main clause:

The girl glanced nervously around her.

Use some of these additional clauses, or invent your own.

  seeming scared of someone

  who was moving quickly through the crowd

  she seemed scared of someone

  as she moved quickly through the crowd

> **Top tip**
>
> 'Coordinating' refers to things that are of equal importance. Coordinating conjunctions are words like 'and', 'but', 'or'.
>
> 'Subordinating' refers to something that is less important than something else. Subordinating conjunctions include 'because', 'although', 'if'.

A *phrase* is a group of connected words that expand on a single word (the 'head').

Noun phrases

Phrases with a noun as their head are noun phrases. A noun phrase is usually a noun with determiners and/or adjectives. For example:

The noisy dragon

The small blue ball

A noun phrase cannot stand by itself as a sentence.

3 Look at the sentences below. Identify the words that make up the noun phrases by replacing them with a pronoun. For example: 'The little girl pelted across the grass.' becomes 'She pelted across it.'

a) Listening to the old man tell his extremely long and drawn-out story had worn Ciara out completely.

b) As the exhausted-looking woman and her chattering daughter passed the market stalls, the girl began to whine.

4 Now look at the sentences below. Replace the highlighted nouns, noun phrases and pronouns with extended noun phrases to add some detail to the sentences. For example: 'The boy held his mother's hand.' could become 'The sweet little boy...'

a) A woman **stopped to buy** apples.

b) She **gazed out of** the window.

Verb phrases

A verb phrase contains one or more verbs and sometimes an adverb. Verbs often occur in *verb chains*, consisting of a main verb (the one telling you what action or process is happening) and one or more auxiliary verbs:

The teacher was marking the exam papers.

We are going to the zoo.

The auxiliary verb in the verb phrase can be a modal verb:

She might leave the room.

You must be hungry.

Verbs and verb phrases must always agree with the *subject* of a sentence. For example, if the subject is plural, the verb or verb phrase must take its plural form.

> **Top tip**
>
> As well as making verbs agree with their subject, it is important to keep an eye on the tenses in your writing, as these must remain consistent. Do not switch between the past and the present without good reason.

5 The table below shows different versions of three phrases. In which version of each sentence does the verb phrase agree with the subject?

He was talking so quickly...	He were talking so quickly...
Each of the students is responsible for...	Each of the students are responsible for...
There's loads of problems...	There are loads of problems...

Which of these clauses can go together? Use the verbs to guide you in making your choices.

If I had more money	I could have done more interesting things
If I had had more money,	I will do more interesting things
If I get more money	I could do more interesting things

Using what you have learned about clauses and phrases in this topic, write the opening paragraph to a letter complaining about something in your school or college. This could be uniform policy, canteen provision, or sports or music facilities.

Checklist for success

✔ Use effective noun phrases to express your concerns (for example: 'the terrible state of the school gym...')

✔ Pay attention to subjec–verb agreement.

✔ Use a range of sentence types with different clauses.

Check your progress:
....

Sound progress ⟫⟫

I can create noun phrases that provide detail.

I can select different clause types to build up interesting sentences.

Excellent progress ⟫⟫⟫

I can use interesting and effective noun phrases.

I can combine clauses effectively into varied sentences.

Understand sentence structures

You will learn how to

- use sentences with different grammatical functions
- build different sentence types using a range of clause types and conjunctions.

Understanding how to construct sentences of different types – and being able to identify and use different sentence functions – will help you produce varied and interesting writing.

Getting you thinking

There are two main ways to categorise sentences: by their function or by their type.

This table shows the four main functions of sentences.

Function	Description	Examples
Statement (declarative)	Requires a subject (pronoun or noun phrase), which generally comes before the verb	I hope to be there on time. Too many people are suffering for us to ignore them.
Command (imperative)	Has no subject; usually begins with a verb	Act now to obtain your free copy. Click below for more information.
Question (interrogative)	Often starts with a wh word or a verb; the main verb may come before the subject	What time shall we meet? Is it time to go yet?
Exclamation (exclamatory)	Not a complete sentence; omits a required element such as a main verb	What a disaster! Not on your life!

1 Identify the functions of these sentences.

a) Put down your pens.

b) What does the writer mean by this line?

c) I am waiting for an answer.

d) What a weird response!

Glossary

wh word: a set of pronouns and adverbs used to form questions, most of which begin with 'wh'.

Pronouns: who, which, what.

Adverbs: where, why, when, how.

Exploring the skills

Sentences can also be categorised by type – that is, according to their structure.

Simple sentences

Simple sentence = main clause:

Simple sentences make strong statements. ——— main clause

In article writing, simple sentences are often used to open paragraphs, as they can provide a clear statement.

 2 Plan an article of five paragraphs on why a charity providing education to poor children in developing countries is a good idea. Your plan should consist of a simple sentence that could open each paragraph.

Compound sentences

Compound sentence = main clause + main clause:

main clause

Compound sentences are formed of two (or more) main clauses **and** they allow you to present two ideas of equal value.

main clause

When writing argument texts and speeches, compound sentences are a good way to present a balance or contrast.

Coordinating conjunctions can be used to connect one main clause to another, or you can use a semicolon instead of a conjunction.

> We have always supported the NHS in the past; we continue to support it now.
>
> Animal welfare is an important concern but isn't the welfare of humans more important?

Coordinating conjunctions	
and	but
both...and	neither...nor
or	yet

3 Write three compound sentences that show a contrast or a balance. Choose from these topics: animal testing, teenage crime, recycling, poverty, exam pressure.

Developing the skills

Complex sentences

Complex sentence = main clause + subordinate clause:

subordinate clause

Complex sentences, including one or more subordinate clauses, allow you to add detail to a main clause.

main clause

Complex sentences are crucial for adding detail. Placing additional clauses into a sentence can make your meaning clearer, by providing explanation or context.

Here are some useful types of subordinate clause.

Clause type	Example
Comment	I think (that)
	as can be seen from the evidence
Condition	if he had listened the first time
	if I were you
Purpose	to get a better view
	in order to have enough time
Reason	because he wanted to
	as we only had one chance
Relative	who was the last to join in
	which was a shame
Result	so some of us waited behind
	and as a result they all failed

Top tip

A main clause can always stand by itself as a simple sentence, but subordinate clauses rely on a main clause to make up a sentence.

Subordinating conjunctions join subordinate clauses to main clauses.

Subordinating conjunctions			
although	because	if	unless
since	whereas	while	when
until	so (that)	as	even if
before	whenever	wherever	whether

4 Which conjunctions could you use to join some of the following clauses as sentences?

My school is huge.   The corridors are always busy.

My school has over 3000 students.   I got lost several times in my first week.

I really like my school now.   It is a very friendly school.

5 Look at this opening to a speech expressing opinions about the testing of cosmetics on animals.

a) What is the effect of each of the clauses in red?

b) If you remove each of these clauses from the sentence, how is the meaning affected?

c) Which ones can you most easily miss out? What kinds of clause are they?

It is, I would argue, wrong to test cosmetics on animals. Since animals depend on us for their care and basic needs, using them for this purpose is abuse. They are not our tools to do with as we please. I would not be as strongly opposed to this practice if there were no other way of testing. However, there is an alternative. Many medical tests, which surely require similar circumstances, are conducted on humans or using artificial methods.

6 Starting with the simple sentence below, find different ways to make it compound and complex. How many different sentences can you build from this one in three minutes? Use conjunctions and different clause types from the previous activities, as well as your own ideas.

Bullying is an important issue.

7 Write a paragraph about your favourite film, television programme or computer game, using one of each type of sentence.

Applying the skills

Read this opening to the novel *Of Mice and Men*.

A few miles south of Soledad, the Salinas River drops in close to the hillside bank and runs deep and green. The water is warm too, for it has slipped twinkling over the yellow sands in the sunlight before reaching the narrow pool. On one side of the river the golden foothill slopes curve up to the strong and rocky Gabilan Mountains, but on the valley side the water is lined with trees – willows fresh and green with every spring, carrying in their lower leaf junctures the debris of the winter's flooding; and sycamores with mottled, white, recumbent limbs and branches that arch over the pool.

John Steinbeck, *Of Mice and Men*

8 Find the main clause(s) in each sentence and then identify three further clauses or phrases in the text.

9 Using different sentence types, write a similar descriptive paragraph about a place you know well, which could open a story and set the scene.

Check your progress:

Sound progress »

I can identify the main clauses in Steinbeck's sentences.

I can include simple, compound and complex sentences to make my writing engaging.

Excellent progress »»

I can identify the types of some individual clauses in the extract.

I can use a range of subordinate clauses to vary the structures in my writing.

Use punctuation accurately

You will learn how to

- use a range of punctuation accurately to engage the reader, including sentence punctuation, speech punctuation and apostrophes.

Punctuation is used to either link or separate grammatical units. The different symbols indicate different degrees of connection or separation. Punctuation can signpost pauses, clarify ideas and alter the tone of your writing.

Getting you thinking

1 Read the texts below and identify all the types of punctuation used.

> 'That's it!' She slammed the door behind her. 'I've had absolutely enough! If she thinks I'm backing down...' She paused, breathing heavily, her anger preventing her from continuing.

> It is important to support animal charities because the whole ecosystem is fragile and delicately balanced. Do you think it won't matter if snow leopards die out? Well, have you thought about the role the snow leopards might play in the food chain overall? You should!

2 Some punctuation is absolutely necessary and some adds interest to the writing. Which do you think is which in these examples? What is the effect of the choices?

3 In each row of the table below, one example uses correct punctuation and the other does not. Which is correct?

,	It is getting dark now, we should leave.	As it is getting dark now, we should leave.
;	I am busy with revision; I can't go out tonight.	I am busy with revision; so I can't go out tonight.
:	There are two things I know about this issue: it's a problem for families, and it's getting worse.	The two things I know about this issue are: it's a problem for families, and it's getting worse.

Top tip

A comma is *never* used between two main clauses.

A semicolon is *never* used to join two main clauses as well as a conjunction.

Here are the main punctuation marks and their functions.

Punctuation	Mark	Purpose	Example
Comma	,	Used to separate items in a list	sun, sea and sand
		Used after a subordinate clause or a phrase at the start of a sentence	To be on time, try catching an earlier bus.
		Used to separate an embedded clause from the main clause	I think, although I could be wrong, that we should act now.
		Used inside speech marks if no other punctuation is required	'I'm leaving now,' he said.
Full stop	.	Used at the end of most sentences	Getting punctuation right is very important.
		Used inside speech marks to show that spoken words are the end of the sentence	He said, 'I'm leaving now.'
Question mark	?	Used to close a sentence that is a question	Can you help?
		Used inside speech marks to show that spoken words are a question	'Are you going now?' he said.
Exclamation mark	!	Used at the end of a sentence to indicate emphasis or volume	Just do it!
		Used inside speech marks to show that spoken words are emphasised or shouted	'I'm leaving now!' he said.
Apostrophe	'	Used for omission and/or contraction	isn't (the 'o' is missing from 'not')
		Used with an 's' to show possession	the Queen's crown
Speech marks	' ' or " "	Used to mark out words that are spoken or quoted	'I'm leaving now,' he said.
Colon	:	Used to introduce a list	I've got everything, I think: purse, keys and phone.
		Used to introduce a definition, elaboration or explanation	I've eaten it all: everything that was left for me.
Semicolon	;	Used to separate items in a list if they are phrases rather than words	the shifting sands; the unrelenting sun; the crowds of tourists
		Used to separate two main clauses instead of a conjunction	It was the hottest summer on record; I'd had enough.
Hyphen	-	Used to join two words together as a compound word	red-bricked
Dash	–	Used to separate an embedded clause from the main clause	I think – although I could be wrong – that we should act now.
		Used to show interruption or pause in direct speech	'I just don't –'
Brackets	( )	Used to separate an embedded clause Used the main clause	I think (although I could be wrong) that we should act now.

Direct speech

You will use direct speech when writing narratives, but you may also find it helpful in articles in which the words of an expert might add weight to your argument (see right).

> **1** Imagine you are writing an article on a local issue – graffiti. You have the following points that you want to make and a quotation from a local resident. Put them together into a paragraph, making sure that you punctuate the quotation accurately.

According to expert Dr Savita Desai, this is only the beginning. 'Climate-change science shows us,' Desai said, 'that weather patterns can get quite bizarre.'

> All graffiti cleaned off last week – now back again.
>
> Expletives sprayed on the wall and insults aimed at the police.
>
> Bob Jones, 63: It's disgusting. Kids play around here and you wouldn't want them seeing this filth.

Apostrophes

Apostrophes are used to show either omission or possession.

> **1** For each of these examples, explain the apostrophe's purpose.
>
> a) What's the point?
>
> b) The writer's use of imagery...
>
> c) I simply don't understand
>
> d) He shouldn't have done that
>
> e) Boys' sports are well catered for
>
> f) The text's point is clear

> **Top tip**
>
> it's = it is
>
> its = belonging to it

Apostrophe + s, used to show possession, is probably the most commonly misused form.

> **6** Which of these usages are correct? Why are the incorrect usages wrong? Explain the purpose of the additional s in these cases.
>
> a) Brooks's use of language...
>
> b) Shakespeare's use of rhyme...
>
> c) Gadgets are not just boy's toys...
>
> d) We took our's home...
>
> e) There are many reason's...
>
> f) The dog bared it's teeth...

> **Top tip**
>
> Omission: cannot – can't
>
> Possession: the pen belonging to Lily – Lily's pen
>
> the pens belonging to the girls – the girls' pens
>
> the pen belonging to Lily Jones – Lily Jones's pen

Developing the skills

Commas, brackets and dashes

Using parenthesis or embedded clauses between pairs of commas, brackets or dashes can give your writing a lively tone, which is particularly useful in some kinds of articles, travel writing and reviews.

7 Compare these pairs of sentences. Which of each pair do you prefer? Why?

a) Although my trip was certainly interesting – who doesn't love having a good story to tell? – I couldn't really recommend it.

Although my trip was certainly interesting, I couldn't really recommend it. But who doesn't love having a good story to tell?

b) That book about the boy who's really a spy is very good.

That book (the one about the boy who's really a spy) is very good.

c) People who do dangerous sports for a hobby are, I would say, completely mad.

I would say that people who do dangerous sports for a hobby are completely mad.

Applying the skills

Look at this GCSE-style task:

A website about holidaying in the UK is collecting entertaining articles for a column entitled 'I Should Have Stayed at Home'. They are looking for light-hearted pieces that relate negative (but not disastrous) experiences on overseas trips. Write an article for this website describing such an experience and explaining your feelings about it.

8 Write the first two paragraphs for this article, ensuring that you include a range of punctuation in your writing.

Check your progress:

Sound progress

I can include apostrophes, commas, full stops and question marks accurately in my article.

I can give my article a light-hearted tone.

Excellent progress

I can use a range of punctuation accurately, including in direct speech, to create particular effects.

I can create an engaging tone in my article using parenthesis and embedded clauses.

Use paragraphs effectively

You will learn how to

- construct a paragraph effectively
- link paragraphs into whole texts.

Paragraphs are the last and largest building block to be considered here. Using them carefully will help you structure and organise your writing.

Getting you thinking

1 Which of these factors are reasons to start a new paragraph?

a) You're writing about a different topic or sub-topic.

b) You've written 10 lines.

c) You haven't started a new paragraph for a while.

d) You're writing about a different time.

e) You're writing about a different place.

f) You're writing about a different person or using a different speaker.

Exploring the skills

Paragraphs help you organise your ideas and guide your reader through your writing. Paragraphs usually focus on one idea each. They use a *topic sentence* that expresses that idea clearly while the rest of the paragraph offers evidence or further detail.

Look at this example of the beginning of an argument text (an opinion article). The topic sentences are in red.

School uniforms should be a thing of the past. They belong in a dusty old cupboard, along with the cane and chalk. Although many would argue otherwise, they do not contribute to discipline and order, but cause discipline problems. **1**

How do they cause discipline problems? Having strict rules about clothing leads to students breaking these rules in a multitude of ways. Ties tied too loosely, shirts not tucked in, skirts of the wrong length: these are all little rebellions against the uniform code. **2**

1 The opening paragraph clearly sets out the writer's views in a broad and general way, while also setting the tone of the article by using strong terms and seeking to engage the reader directly.

2 The second paragraph focuses specifically on one aspect of the argument and offers evidence for that claim.

Furthermore, these little rebellions lead to unnecessary clashes between teachers and students, and waste class time. Many lessons in schools that are strict about their uniform policy begin with a series of instructions or even sanctions related to uniform rules. **3**

3 The third paragraph picks up the evidence and develops a further argument from it.

Cohesion

In all extended writing, it is important that paragraphs are linked together and follow on logically from one another. This is a key way to achieve cohesion in your writing – producing a piece of text that hangs together and flows fluently.

Cohesive devices include

- pronouns linking to previous statements (the problem is simple... / Although it seems...)

- conjunctions and **adverbials** making links (the problem is simple... / Although it seems...)

- repetition of key words and phrases (the problem is simple... / Although the problem seems...)

2 In the opinion article example, look closely at how the paragraphs link to each other. What language devices provide connections from one paragraph to the next?

Developing the skills

3 Look at this extract taken from the first draft of a book review. How would you divide this into paragraphs? Are there different possibilities here?

The author has nailed everything about this book. It's the perfect opener for a trilogy: it sets up a truly epic battle whilst still having a complete and resolved story arc in this instalment. It's also a skilful urban fantasy, bringing fantasy elements to life in a fully realistic contemporary UK setting. That realistic setting is one of the novel's core strengths. I also noticed the voice and tone of narration and the dialogue, all of which completely ring true for contemporary teens. The fantasy elements are pretty unusual and make a lot of demands on the reader (and characters!) in terms of suspension of disbelief,

(continued)

Glossary

adverbial: a word or phrase used like an adverb to modify a verb or clause

therefore, the novel's realism for the 'urban' side is essential. I wanted to say I loved all the characters, but maybe that would mislead you. I mean I appreciate how well drawn they are as characters. Trust me, the baddies are plenty bad enough to not be 'loved'! Again, the author's ear for dialogue helps a lot here, and Mio's voice as narrator is an easy shortcut into her mind, enabling us to easily be fully on her side. The trilogy centres on Mio's sword, so there are plenty of fight scenes and risks to life and limb. Things move along at a good pace for an action-type fantasy, and there is tension and danger aplenty. At the same time, a romance subplot is bubbling up and clearly sowing seeds to be developed later in the trilogy. The key ingredients of a great urban fantasy are all here.

4 Plan an article in which you argue your views on an issue you feel strongly about. For example, you could write about:

- the use of airbrushing to present models and celebrities unrealistically

- the pressures of exams on teenagers

- the popularity of 'reality television'.

To do this, you will need to

a) decide on five key points you want to make

b) put your five points in a sensible order

c) for each key point, construct a clear simple sentence that summarises that point (a topic sentence)

d) decide which (if any) **connectives** to use in each of your simple sentences, either from the prompts below or from your own ideas.

first, second	clearly, obviously
it is evident/noteworthy that	furthermore, moreover
we must also consider	an additional factor is

Glossary
....

connective: conjunctions and conjunctive adverbs used to show links between parts of a text

5 Select one of your topic sentences and develop it into a full paragraph, remembering to use varied sentences and to stick to one topic for the whole paragraph. You could expand on your topic sentence by

a) offering evidence such as statistics or an anecdote

b) explaining your point more fully and in more detail

c) making a comparison to something else – for example, comparing different time periods or different countries

d) acknowledging an opposing view (a counter-argument) and arguing against it.

6 Select another of your sentences and work it into a new paragraph, but this time use your topic sentence to **close** the paragraph – effectively summarising the point you have just made.

As well as linking ideas by using connectives, sentences and paragraphs need to show coherence and cohesion in other ways, too. For example, the tense and point of view you use should be consistent both within and between paragraphs.

Rewrite this paragraph to make it clearer and more consistent.

> She paused for breath, looking around to check where she is now. Suddenly she realises she didn't know this place at all; she's never been there before. Panic gripped her and she didn't know what to do next. Who could help her? Glancing around, she sees a woman with a small child and decides to ask her for directions.

Top tip

Topic sentences do not always fall at the start of paragraphs, but a new paragraph should open in a way that justifies starting a new paragraph.

Check your progress:

Sound progress

I can use one paragraph for each idea, clearly indicated in my topic sentences.

I can write using connectives, pronouns and tenses accurately.

Excellent progress

My paragraphs all open clearly, providing signposts for my reader, and there is variety in my paragraph openings.

I can write consistently and cohesively, using a wide range of devices.

Applying the skills

'Modern music is all the same; it lacks innovation and creativity.'

Write a letter to a newspaper responding to this headline. You must argue either for or against this viewpoint. Pay particular attention to the structure of your letter as a whole and your use of paragraphs.

Check your progress

Sound progress

- [ ] I understand what nouns, verbs, adjectives and adverbs are.
- [ ] I can conjugate regular verbs.
- [ ] I can identify main and subordinate clauses.
- [ ] I can use simple noun phrases and verb phrases.
- [ ] I can identify and use simple and compound sentences.
- [ ] I can use some different clause types and conjunctions.
- [ ] I can use apostrophes, commas, full stops and any exclamation or question marks accurately.
- [ ] I can use at least one type of less common punctuation correctly, such as a semicolon, dashes or brackets.
- [ ] I can construct a paragraph around a topic sentence.
- [ ] I know when to start a new paragraph.

Excellent progress

- [ ] I understand the characteristics of each of the eight word classes.
- [ ] I can conjugate regular and irregular verbs.
- [ ] I can use main and subordinate clauses accurately and effectively.
- [ ] I can use extended noun phrases and verb phrases.
- [ ] I can use simple, compound and complex sentences.
- [ ] I can incorporate a variety of clause types and conjunctions in my writing.
- [ ] I can use punctuation accurately, including in direct speech, to create particular effects.
- [ ] I can use parenthesis and/or subordinate clauses to create a chatty tone, with accurate punctuation.
- [ ] I can vary the position of topic sentences in paragraphs.
- [ ] I can link paragraphs cohesively.

What's it all about?

Writing to inform and explain is about being clear and accurate in what you say, and making sure the reader can follow stages in a process or understand the reasons you give. It is also about providing appropriate detail for the task and audience.

This chapter will show you how to

- use precise and appropriate vocabulary
- write sentences for clarity, sequence and purpose
- use punctuation, prepositions and prepositional phrases to explain clearly
- select different tenses and modal forms to hypothesise and give reasons
- use a range of paragraph styles, including those with topic sentences, to provide information.

You will write

- an article about the history of the smartphone
- a newspaper report about the theft of the *Mona Lisa*
- a tourist leaflet containing details about a ghost walk or history trail
- an article about the dangers of internet shopping
- an article about the history and practice of commercial whaling.

Use precise and appropriate vocabulary

You will learn how to

- use formal, specialist or informal vocabulary appropriately
- select adverbs and adverbials for explaining time, place and process.

In writing to inform and explain, the vocabulary you use must suit your task and audience. By choosing an appropriate degree of formality and by selecting words that describe processes and situations, you can be certain that the reader will understand what you write.

Getting you thinking

Read these two short texts, both about a new camera app.

App reviews: Piccy-Plus

Find out what our reviewer thought about Piccy-Plus – a new app to wow your mates or get ready for a night out.

Let's face it – you don't want to worry that your eyes will be redder than your outfit in those pics. And you wanna make sure you look fab at that party when you post them online.

Piccy-Plus reckon they've got those problems totally sorted with their app for your phone. It's got loads of features to glam you up, like 'make-up magic', and you can change the style to suit your style. At 99p, we think it's the best we've seen for that amount of cash.

Piccy-Plus 1.2   **£0.99**
*****

Details   Reviews   Related

Improve images in an instant

Piccy-Plus makes photos perfect with new key features such as advanced editing with crop and red-eye reduction.

- Super zoom: wider shots than in version 1
- Range of 30 effects including sepia, retro, neon and fish-eye
- New 'make-up magic' feature
- Video or camera options
- Manual and auto settings
- Instant upload

Developer: PiccyPic
Category: Photo and Video
Updated: October 2013

1 Both texts deal with the same app, but what is different about how they are written?

a) Think about the points below and note down your ideas:
- the information each text provides
- the language each text uses
- how information is presented and organised in each text.

b) What do you think is the *purpose* of each text? (For example, is it to inform, explain, persuade?) Who is the intended *audience* for each text?

Exploring the skills

Formal language is language that uses standard, professional-sounding words and phrases. *Informal language* means words and phrases in a more chatty style that you might use when speaking to friends, for example.

Find the **synonyms** for these words and phrases from the first text:

a) impress

b) friends

c) believe

d) have the best solution

e) numerous.

Find any words or phrases that have been shortened in the first text (such as 'they've').

Decide if the synonyms and shortened words you have found are formal or informal. What does this tell us about the tone of the first text? (Is it friendly, serious, business-like, chatty or thoughtful?)

Now look at the second text. List any specialist vocabulary from the **lexicon** of camera applications (such as 'editing'). Is there more of this vocabulary in the first or second text? Why do you think this is?

5 How does each text refer to the reader/audience? For example, which one uses the *pronoun* 'you' and **possessive** 'your'?

Write one or two paragraphs comparing the two texts. Comment on which you think is more informative and which is more persuasive. Consider the levels of formality used in each and say something about the target audience.

Glossary

synonyms: words or phrases that are close to or identical in meaning to each other

lexicon: a bank of words often used in connection with a topic or situation – for example, words and phrases such as 'penalty', 'corner', 'tackle', 'playing too deep' or 'getting stuck in' are all used in a sporting context

possessive: 'my', 'your', 'our' and so on are possessive determiners – they tell/determine who something belongs to (for example, '*my* book')

Developing the skills

When you explain why or how a process occurs, you also need to make sure the *detail* and *information* you provide are clearly expressed.

Adverbs and *adverbials* tell you how, when or where something happened:

'totally sorted' ————————————————— how

'you'll want to look fab at that party' ———— where

'post the pics online later on' ————————— when

Adverbials are usually phrases or clauses that act like adverbs:

'Put the gift on the table.' ———— adverbial
———— verb

Adjectives add more detail to nouns to make *noun phrases*:

'new, key features'. ———— adjective
———— adjective

Read this opening to a biographical text about the Nazi photographer Leni Riefenstahl.

Innovative filmmaker and Nazi propagandist, Berta Helene Amalie Riefenstahl was born into a prosperous, cultured family and began her artistic career as a dancer. Although she was highly regarded on the Berlin stage, a knee injury put an end to her aspirations.

In the 1920s she turned to acting, taking part in the 'mountain films' of Arnold Fanck. By the time of Adolf Hitler's ascendance, she had directed a mountain film of her own, 'The Blue Light', breaking boundaries for women in that period.

Her great opportunity to make a breakthrough came in 1934, when she was invited, with a limitless budget, to photograph the annual Nazi rally. From this came 'Triumph of the Will, one of Riefenstahl's seminal pieces, and a key work in the history of film, in terms of technical innovation.

'Triumph of the Will' was also a crucial component of Hitler's propaganda campaign, fuelling accusations, which Riefenstahl consistently denied, that she was a Nazi sympathiser.

Leni Riefenstahl biography from the History Channel website

7 Note down the adverbs or adverbials that will help you answer these questions:

a) How did Leni Riefenstahl begin her career?

b) Where was she 'highly regarded'?

c) When did she turn to acting?

8 List the adjectives that will help you answer these questions:

a) What sort of filmmaker was she?

b) What was her family like?

c) What was her budget for the photography for the Nazi rally in 1934?

Applying the skills

9 Imagine it is 2042. It's been 50 years since the invention of the smartphone and it is now a thing of the past. Write a short article about smartphones for an online magazine aimed at adults.

a) Briefly explain what a smartphone is.

b) Inform readers about its history/development using the fact file below.

c) Mention the important brands in the smartphone's history.

d) Explain what replaced it (make this bit up!).

Fact file

1992 First smartphone invented by IBM. Nicknamed 'Simon', features include calendar, address book, calculator, email service and touch screen. Cost: about £600.

1996 Nokia launches series of smartphones, basically a cross between a mobile and a PDA (Personal Digital Assistant).

2000 R380 from Ericsson – touch screen and foldable keyboard. First device to be called a 'smartphone'.

2002 Smartphone revolution begins – e.g. Blackberry. New features include MP3 player, camera and wireless technology. Exchange Email also popular.

2007 Apple's iPhone introduced with huge App Store.

2008 Phones using open-source, Android operating system start to take off, e.g. ones by Google, Intel and HTC.

2013 New smartphones constantly being introduced, aiming for faster internet speeds; hybrid gadgets (such as 'watch-phones') developed.

Checklist for success

✔ Use an appropriate level of formality in your vocabulary.

✔ Use a range of adverbs and adverbials to help explain the history and development of the smartphone.

✔ Use noun phrases and the lexicon of smartphones to describe their features and uses.

Check your progress:

Sound progress

I can generally use the right level of formality in my article.

I can use some specific vocabulary to do with smartphones.

I can use adverbs accurately to add further detail.

Excellent progress

I can keep appropriate formality throughout my article.

I can use technical or specific vocabulary appropriately.

I can use adverbs, adverbials and noun phrases confidently.

Write sentences for clarity, sequence and purpose

You will learn how to

- use and sequence different sentence types to inform and explain effectively
- select the passive or active voice according to the context and purpose.

The types of sentences you choose, and the order in which they appear, can make a big difference to the clarity of your text. The purpose of your writing should also help you decide whether to write in the active or passive voice.

Getting you thinking

Read this short crime report.

> I unlocked the door and entered the room. Jeff and Jenny lay dead in a pool of water. There was broken glass all around them and the window was open. The murderer had escaped.

1 Consider the following questions:

a) What types of sentences have been used in this crime report – *simple*, *compound* or *complex* (see page 11)?

b) Why do you think this is?

c) Who do you think the criminal is, and what has happened?

Exploring the skills

Writing to inform: The report above is an example of an *informative* text. When reporting the simple facts of a crime, information needs to be crystal clear. Simple and compound sentences help to give information in a clear and focused way.

Writing to explain: Explanatory texts go further. They present information but they also explain or interpret that information. To do this, you may need a greater variety of sentence types. These could be compound sentences with coordinated main clauses, complex sentences with main and subordinate clauses (see pages 10–11), or a combination of both patterns, like the example below.

There was broken glass all around them and the window was open, which suggested the crime was opportunistic rather than planned.

two simple sentence are joined together with 'and' to make a basic compound sentence...

... but the writer adds a subordinate clause, explaining the event

Read this extract from a newspaper article.

Diamonds are forever – but gang stole £32m worth in three minutes

It was all over in three minutes. **1** That was all the time it took eight highly professional thieves disguised as policemen and armed with machine guns fitted with laser sights to break on to the **apron** at Zaventem, Belgium's biggest airport, on Monday night, race up to a Swiss plane about to be cleared for take-off, remove diamonds weighing 22lbs and worth about $50m (£32m), and speed away. **2**

No shots were fired and no one was injured. The first the 22 passengers knew of the heist was when their flight was cancelled a short while later.

Last night Antwerp, the world's oldest and biggest diamond-trading centre, was in shock at the ease with which one of the biggest diamond robberies in history had been carried out. Caroline de Wolf, spokesperson for the Antwerp World Diamond Centre, said: 'Antwerp is the most highly secured diamond centre in the industry, guaranteeing a safe business environment and safe transport of the vast stream of valuable goods to and from Antwerp.'

'We find it hard to understand how a robbery such as yesterday's could take place.'

To minimise exposure to theft it is usual to move diamonds by air and to load them into the hold of aircraft as late as possible before take-off. But these precautions were to no avail on Monday.

Peter Popham, *The Independent*, Tuesday 19 February 2013

1 Short simple sentence neatly sums up focus of text to come and makes us ask 'What?'

2 Long complex sentence containing a range of actions ('race up' and so on), adverbials ('on Monday night') and noun phrases ('biggest airport').

Glossary

apron: the paved strip around buildings at an airport

2 What information are you given in the second sentence?

3 The second paragraph consists of a compound sentence followed by a complex one. Why do you think the writer began with the compound sentence?

4 How is the text *sequenced*? Look at the key *adverbial of time* in the first paragraph – 'on Monday night'. What further references to time can you identify in the following four paragraphs?

Top tip

Use longer simple, compound or complex sentences to follow up shorter ones with explanation and detail.

5 Identify the simple, compound and complex sentences in the paragraph below, then reorganise it in the order that works best. Use the adverbials of time to help you sequence the paragraph.

> From that moment, there was never a chance the police would recover the jewels, despite extensive use of road-blocks, enquiries and conversations with underworld contacts. The gang simply disappeared into thin air. Their escape route had been well planned and they left no evidence behind them.

Developing the skills

The active and passive voices also play a role in the article.

- The *active voice* is used when the subject (the 'doer' of the action) is mentioned, and what he/she/it does is made clear. For example: 'The police (subject) chased (verb) the thieves (object)'.

- An example of the *passive voice* might be: 'The thieves were chased by the police' or 'The thieves were chased'. The thieves become the *subject* of the sentence, but the form is passive because the thieves are not *doing* the chasing, but 'receiving' it.

Here are some extracts from later in the article. Note down whether they are active or passive and explain the reason for or effect of this choice.

Sentence	Active or passive	Reason/effect
'Four men wearing masks and hooded police cagoules leapt out of each vehicle and held pilots, crew and other personnel at gunpoint while they removed the precious load.'	Active	Gives a dramatic account of events and what was done
'A Mercedes van was later found burnt out.'		
'The gang broke through the airport's security fence at a point between two construction sites.'		

Look at the sentence below. Does it use the active or passive voice? Why did the writer choose to put it like this?

> No shots were fired and no one was injured.

8 Here are three different headlines for the article. In each case, what is the effect of moving words to the front of the headline?

Jewels worth £32 million stolen in three minutes

Gang steals jewels worth £32 million in three minutes

Thieves net more than £10 million a minute in airport heist

 9 Look again at the headlines above. Think about whether they are active or passive, then choose the one you would use. Why did you make this choice?

Applying the skills

10 Here is some information about a crime. Using these facts, write two paragraphs of a newspaper report that uses simple, compound and complex sentences to *explain how* and *why* the crime may have taken place.

Fact file

Crime: Theft of the *Mona Lisa* from the Louvre Paris.

When? Stolen between 7 and 8 on Monday morning. Usual guard for the room on holiday; replacement left his position for a few minutes to smoke a cigarette.

Evidence: The frame left in a stairwell, no fingerprints.

How discovered? A researcher, Louis Beroud, noticed it was missing when he came to look at it.

Who? Sixty investigators involved in tracing the criminal. Police suspect an employee may be responsible, as museum was closed at that time.

Motive: Unlikely to be financial. Impossible to sell, so political?

Checklist for success

✔ Use simple or compound sentences to state most certain or most important facts.

✔ Use complex sentences to add further detail, explanation and interpretation.

✔ Consider using the passive voice where you don't know the 'agent' (the 'doer' of the action) or where the subject is less important than what has been done (for example, think about how you would write about the frame in the stairwell).

Check your progress:

Sound progress

I can use a range of sentence types to make clear the most important facts of the case.

I can use the active voice to describe the events of the theft.

Excellent progress

I can use the three sentence types to explain information in ways appropriate to the context of the article.

I can choose between the active and passive voice to highlight key facts.

Use punctuation, prepositions and prepositional phrases to explain clearly

You will learn how to

- use prepositions and prepositional phrases to explain processes clearly
- use colons to introduce explanations and reasons
- use commas in lists and to mark off details.

Our language offers a range of tools, including punctuation and prepositions, to help you explain processes or the relationships between things clearly.

Getting you thinking

Read this incomplete short spy message.

> Leave the briefcase _____ the ledge _____ the front wall of Number 7, Bond Street, then wait _____ the tube station.

1 Why do the missing words make this set of instructions confusing? What type of words are missing?

Now read this second set of instructions.

> After Boris Martin and Zak arrive drive them to the car park under the sign for the exit.

2 How does the lack of punctuation create confusion here?

Exploring the skills

3 Rewrite the messages above, adding the following words and forms of punctuation:

a) prepositions or prepositional phrases such as *inside*, *at the end of*, *under*, *behind*

b) commas to separate items in a list.

c) conjunctions such as *and*.

4 Write brief instructions for someone who has never been into your classroom before on where to place a hidden camera. Use *adverbs* and *adverbials of time* or *sequence* – such as 'Next' and 'After that' – to help your reader understand what to do. Begin:

> Follow these simple steps in order to set up the camera: first, _____

Top tip

A *colon* can be useful after an introductory sentence followed by a series of steps.

Now, read this longer text from a tourist brochure about the historical town of Hastings.

prepositional phrase

Park at the top of the West Hill, close to the children's playground, and then make your way down one of the paths across the hill itself. To your right, you will just be able to make out the ruins of the old castle, and the café near to it but above one of the two funicular railways that serve this side of the town. As you reach the end of the path, you will see signs to your left pointing towards the 'Smugglers' Adventure': this is a warren of caves, grottoes, nooks and crannies under the hill featuring lifelike representations of battles between customs men and the smugglers themselves.

Before you descend the steps to the Old Town and its quaint shops and galleries, pause for a moment to take in the view: the tall black fishermen's huts by the beach, the other cliff railway on the East Hill, and the sea itself, stretching to Eastbourne and beyond to the west.

5 Identify the prepositions and prepositional phrases used to clarify where things are in relation to one another.

6 There are also some adverbials and conjunctions here that help describe the chronological sequence. Find these in the text.

7 The text uses colons to provide further explanation or details. What is being explained in each case?

Applying the skills

8 Write a short text (about 150 words) describing a ghost walk or history trail in your local area for a tourist leaflet.

The more interesting and complicated the trail, the better – but however long your trail is, it must be clear and easy to follow. Make up your trail if you wish.

Checklist for success

✔ Use connecting adverbials (such as 'After that…'), prepositions and adverbs to provide clear detail about where things and places are, and the order to follow.

✔ Use colons followed by a list with commas to provide further information.

Check your progress:

Sound progress 》》

I can write instructions for a simple trail in clear steps using separate sentences, and create a list correctly using full stops and commas.

Excellent progress 》》

I can explain an extended trail using full stops, commas and colons, and relevant prepositions and connectives to make the process clear.

Select different tenses and modal forms to hypothesise and give reasons

You will learn how to

- use subordinate clauses to hypothesise and give reasons
- use the present and past perfect tenses with modals to suggest probability or possibility.

You may be asked not only to explain what happened and why, but also to **hypothesise** about what *might* happen in the future. You'll need to use tenses carefully to explain the possible outcomes of actions in the past and present.

Glossary

hypothesise: to suggest a possible outcome based on information about an action

Getting you thinking

Read these statements that hypothesise (make a reasonable prediction) about the future.

- 'If the government acts decisively, war will be avoided.'
- 'If you had told her how you felt, she might have forgiven you!'
- 'If you work harder, you could do better in your exams next time.'

> All these *subordinate clauses* start with 'If', but each one has a slightly different purpose. Identify which one
>
> a) suggests *the possibility* that things might be different now if a different decision *had been made* in the past
>
> b) says that there will be a *definite outcome* in the future if a specific decision *is taken now*
>
> c) says that a future outcome *is possible* (not definite) if someone *changes their behaviour now*.

Exploring the skills

Modal verbs can suggest the weight or likelihood of an occurrence:

If you had told **1** her how you felt, she might **2** have forgiven you!

1 Past perfect form used with 'if' to suggest an action that is over – in this case something that wasn't done.

2 Modal suggest possibility.

> Another modal – *could* – is used in the third sentence. In terms of possibility/probability, where would you place it on the line of probability with these alternatives?

might	*would*	*should*	*ought to*	*will*

possible ———————→ probable ———————→ certain

Developing the skills

Read this dialogue.

Interviewer: Is the decline of the high street inevitable?

Business expert: Not necessarily. If we had supported small local shops in the past when the big chains were taking over, we wouldn't have empty, boarded-up shops now. If we want our high streets to prosper, we need to think about what we can do to save them.

Interviewer: Such as?

Business expert: If we focus on those things that cannot be done online – meeting people face to face, tasting locally produced food, and so on – then we might reinvigorate our local shops.

CLOSING DOWN SALE

> The business expert uses the subordinate clause starting with 'if' plus the **past perfect** tense 'had' to suggest something we should have done in the past. What should or could we have done?

> The business expert uses similar clauses with present tense verbs to hypothesise about the future. Which clauses are they? How certain of the outcome is the expert in each case?

We use the *past perfect* tense for completed actions in the past:

'I walked home and realised I had left my wallet in the shop.'

We use the *present* tense or *present progressive* tense to describe or assert a current situation or problem.

'Young people are exposed daily to expensive goods that are out of their reach, and this is making them envious and acquisitive.'

> How would you rewrite the sentence above using a modal form of 'make' to suggest the outcome is *less* certain?

Glossary

past perfect: the tense used to describe an action that was completed before another action took place

Applying the skills

> Write a newspaper article about the negative consequences of internet shopping on our high streets. How might we change people's behaviour?

Checklist for success

✔ Decide if you are going to assert something strongly (in the present tense) or more tentatively (using modals).

✔ Use the past perfect tense to talk about what we did well or badly in the past.

✔ Use subordinate clauses starting with 'if' to hypothesise about the future.

Check your progress:

Sound progress 〉〉

I can use a range of tenses to explain the history of internet shopping and its dangers.

I can use some modal forms to suggest how things might change in the future.

Excellent progress 〉〉〉

I can use the past perfect, present and present progressive tenses to explain internet shopping and its dangers.

I can use a range of modal forms to speculate on how we might change people's behaviour.

Use a range of paragraph styles, including those with topic sentences, to provide information

You will learn how to

- use topic sentences to move from the general to the specific and vice versa
- use tenses and connectives across paragraphs to help explain a process or give information about a current situation.

You can alter the content, length and sequence of sentences in paragraphs in order to draw the reader's attention to particular information at particular points. You can also give each paragraph a different purpose or focus so that the reader is able to follow your thoughts more easily.

Getting you thinking

Read this paragraph from an article about crocodiles in Australia.

> There are a several signs that crocodiles are more of a danger in Australia's Northern Territories today. For a start, huge numbers now roam the outback since hunting was banned in 1971. Then there's the fact that when the rivers rise, crocs now come into people's backyards looking for prey. Finally, those taking a quick dip in the local pool or lake have found these terrifying predators lurking beneath the surface.

 What is the main focus or idea in the opening paragraph above? How do you know?

 Could the sentences in this paragraph be sequenced differently (without changing the words)? Why? Why not?

Exploring the skills

The *topic sentence* of a paragraph is the sentence that

- tells us what the main focus of the paragraph is
- doesn't go into specific detail.

The topic sentence often comes at the beginning of a paragraph (as in the example above), but it doesn't have to.

Read this later paragraph from the same article.

> Their jaws are as powerful as any in the animal kingdom, and some examples are claimed to be up to 9 metres long. Add to this their swimming prowess and armour-plated bodies. All in all, they are perfectly formed killing machines.

Which is the topic sentence in this paragraph? How do you know?

4 Could the topic sentence be placed elsewhere in the paragraph? Would you have to change any words?

5 Read these further details about crocodiles.

- Indian mugger crocodile known to attack humans.
- Fatal attack on Chinese girl, aged 9, in Guangxi region in 2009.
- 21-foot crocodile captured after several fatal attacks in Philippines, 2011.

What is the common focus of each of these statements?

Write a paragraph of three or four sentences using the details above. Include either a topic sentence that introduces these specific details or a concluding sentence that sums them up.

> **Top tip**
>
> Moving from a general introductory sentence into more specific details, or moving from the specific details to a general summing-up sentence, are both effective ways to provide easy-to-follow information about a topic.

> **Top tip**
>
> Remember to link your sentences using appropriate conjunctions and conjunctive adverbs (see page 24). Make sure you use tenses consistently.

Developing the skills

In informative or explanatory texts you can use topic sentences and sentence order to make your focus clear.

Read this short article about a different type of predator.

This summer, many outdoor events and fairs will feature a display of great skill. A falcon (a type of hawk) will be let loose and then return to its trainer following a series of commands and actions. This dramatic spectacle will entrance spectators, as the falcons swoop down from trees or high in the air to retrieve the morsel of food the falconer offers them. What they will observe is falconry, a centuries-old activity – the act of hunting animals in their natural habitat through the use of a trained bird of prey.

As has been suggested, the process of training hawks is highly skilled. It begins with 'manning' — that is, getting the hawk used to your presence. Once the hawk trusts you and will feed calmly on your gloved fist, training can begin. The hawk now has to learn to come to you for food. First, it needs to be attached to a line – called a 'creance' – and placed on a post or an assistant's hand. Then, you hold a piece of meat in your gloved fist so the hawk can see it. To start with, it will probably come from only a very short distance, but after a few

tense

main topic, showing that this is the topic sentence

(continued)

days you can increase the distance to about 50–100 metres. When the hawk comes this far without hesitation, you are ready to let it fly freely. Then, using a 'lure' (a line with meat at the end) you can train it to follow or come to you.

These specialised methods go back many, many years. In fact, back in the 16th century, Shakespeare wrote a speech in his play *The Taming of the Shrew* in which the main character, Petruchio, talked about how he was going to tame his wife as if she were a hawk! Today, falconry is often used to enthral audiences at exhibitions and even weddings. But, don't forget the ancient skills or training that go into it as you watch such a display this summer.

7 Write answers to these questions in full sentences.

a) What is the main topic or focus of each of these paragraphs?

b) Does each paragraph have a topic sentence? If so, which is it?

c) What are the main tenses used in each paragraph? Why are they different (think about the topic or function of each one)?

d) Paragraph 2 explains a sequence. Which words or phrases tell you this?

8 Look at how the paragraphs in the article are organised.

a) Would these three paragraphs make sense in any order? Why? Why not?

b) How are the paragraphs themselves linked (look at the first sentences of paragraphs 2 and 3)?

c) What is the function of the final sentence of the third paragraph?

Applying the skills

Careful use of paragraphs, what they focus on, and the arrangement of the sentences in them, is vital when explaining a specialised topic.

Look at the three columns of information on the topic of whaling opposite.

The history of whaling	The process	The situation today
Dates back to 3000 BC. First organised whaling fleets in 17th century. In the late 1930s, more than 50 000 whales killed annually. 1986 International Whaling Commission banned commercial whaling. Not all countries signed up to it.	Many different types of whaling – for example, Norwegian whalers catch minke whales by firing harpoons from cannons on bow of boat. Follow up with rifles if not killed immediately. Hunters have to take safety classes and proficiency exam to prove they know how to use weapons. Other methods include beaching whales by driving them onto land.	Some countries, such as Japan, have continued so-called 'scientific research' whaling. Japanese believe whale stocks are now at a level where whaling could start again. Norway and Russia among countries still whaling. Many arguments over whaling, including who should decide whether it is legal, whether the data about stocks is correct, and so on.

9 Write an article about whaling, using at least three paragraphs. Don't present a point of view – just give information about whaling and explain how it has been and is carried out.

Checklist for success

✔ Decide what the function of each of your paragraphs will be. To give the history? To explain a process?

✔ Think about the tenses you will use and how these might help order events chronologically.

✔ Use connectives of time or sequence to help you organise the information.

✔ Consider where the topic sentence might go in each paragraph.

Check your progress:

Sound progress 〉

I can write clear paragraphs, focusing on the history of whaling, the process and the situation today, each with a topic sentence.

I can use tenses correctly in each paragraph.

Excellent progress 〉〉

I can vary where the topic sentence appears in my paragraphs.

I can use tenses and connectives of time to explain the changes that have taken place in whaling.

Check your progress

Sound progress

- I can generally use the right level of formality for the audience or task.
- I can use adverbs accurately to add further detail about where, when and how.
- I can use some subject-specific vocabulary to make explanations clear.
- I can use the active voice to convey straightforward actions.
- I can use a range of sentence types to make important facts clear.
- I can write instructions in clear steps using correct, separate sentences, with full stops and commas in lists.
- I can use tenses correctly, for example the past perfect and present tense, to explain.
- I can use some modal forms to suggest future events and their likelihood.
- I can write clear paragraphs, each with a topic sentence.

Excellent progress

- I can use appropriate formality or informality at all times.
- I can use pronouns, adverbs, adverbials and noun phrases confidently.
- I can use technical or subject-specific vocabulary appropriately.
- I can use the active or passive voice to foreground key information.
- I can use the three sentence types to explain information in ways appropriate to the context.
- I can explain fluently using full stops, commas and colons, and relevant prepositions and connectives.
- I can use tenses and connectives of time coherently to explain a process.
- I can use the past perfect, present and present progressive tenses to explain an issue in a coherent and convincing way.
- I can use a range of modal forms accurately to speculate on the likelihood of future events.
- I can vary where the topic sentence appears in my paragraphs.

Chapter 3
Writing to argue and persuade

What's it all about?

Writing to argue and persuade is about manipulating and influencing your reader's response. In persuasive texts you generally present one clear viewpoint, whereas in argument texts you make reference to both sides of the debate. In both cases, you present these ideas through the power and impact of carefully chosen vocabulary, the structure or sequence of your argument, and the appropriateness of the tone you strike for your audience.

This chapter will show you how to
- select vocabulary to make your viewpoint clear and influence your reader
- use imperative and modal verbs to convey tone and levels of certainty
- use conjunctions and conjunctive adverbs to write coherent arguments
- vary word and clause order in sentences to create particular effects
- vary sentence types to persuade readers
- select punctuation to convey your opinions appropriately
- structure argument and persuasive texts effectively.

You will write
- a letter about the sale of animals from one zoo to another
- an email to a mobile-phone manufacturer
- a speech arguing against the building of a wind farm
- the front page of a health leaflet about fruit juice
- a website home page for a charity supporting street children
- an opinion piece about going to music festivals
- an article arguing for or against horse-racing as a sport.

Select vocabulary to make your viewpoint clear and influence your reader

You will learn how to

- select adverbs, verbs, nouns and adjectives carefully to express your opinion
- expand noun and verb phrases to influence the reader.

When you write to argue or persuade, you need to judge the tone and strength of the language you use to influence your reader, choosing your words precisely to make the right impact.

Getting you thinking

Read this extract from a radio interview about animal rights.

Interviewer: Isn't it fair to say that when you foolishly released wild beasts from the zoo, you completely endangered their lives and the lives of residents in the area?

Protester: I utterly reject that. The ridiculous idea of a tiny, confined space in which you keep defenceless creatures simply for the pleasure of the public is outdated and ill-conceived. Releasing them was simply the only course of action open to us.

 1   What opinions are expressed by the two speakers? How do you know?

 2   How strong are these views? What words do the speakers use to influence the listener?

Exploring the skills

Both the interviewer and the protester use well-chosen words and phrases. In particular, they use two language structures:

- **noun phrases:** 'a tiny, confined space' (adjective + adjective + noun)
- **verbs modified by adverbs:** 'foolishly released' (adverb + verb).

3   Copy and complete the table below to identify at least two more examples of each of these language structures.

Noun phrase	Verb modified by adverb
'a tiny, confined space'	'foolishly released'

4   In each case, what would be the effect of removing the adjectives (before the nouns) or the adverbs (from the verbs)?

Now read a later extract from the same radio programme.
Another speaker is now involved.

Interviewer: Let me bring in Regine Lewis, an expert in animal care and protection. What are your views about the protesters' actions?

Regine: Well, I feel that releasing animals was rather misguided, if understandable. Whatever we feel about zoos, setting free animals that are not native to the UK is a little reckless. Zoos often play a key role in preserving species, and we should reform them not close them down.

5 Identify the adjectives and adverbs in Regine's phrases (one example is 'Zoos *often* play').

6 Copy the scale shown right. Where would you place the protester's and Regine's words about zoos along this line?

1 ——▶ 5 ——▶ 10

| not very strong words | quite strong words | very strong words |

If you want to strengthen the effect of what you say, you can use adverbs like the ones listed right. These are called *intensifiers*.

7 Write a sentence or two explaining how you feel about animal cruelty. Use two of the intensifiers on the right to strengthen your viewpoint.

totally   completely
absolutely   utterly   really
particularly   exceptionally

 You can also use different verbs to express the strength of your feelings. Look at the statements below and allocate a number from 1 (very weak) to 10 (very strong) to rate the strength of feeling in each statement.

Statement	Scale of 1–10
I don't mind seeing animals in captivity.	
I detest watching them do tricks.	
I hate the way they are kept in cages.	
I dislike the idea of zoos.	
I object to spending money to view wild animals.	
I disagree with keeping any animals confined.	

 Write three sentences on a topic you feel strongly about (for example, animal testing, dance music, tattoos) using some of the verbs from the table above.

Try to link clauses or sentences using words such as 'but': for example, 'I hate the look of tattoos, *but* don't mind if people choose to have them.'

Developing the skills

When writing to argue or persuade, you can also make use of positive, negative and **neutral words** to influence your reader.

Read these two versions of the same extract from a campaign leaflet for animal welfare.

neutral words: words that describe an action or thing without expressing a particular point of view

> Kept in a squalid and claustrophobic cage, Eddie was so feeble and scrawny he could no longer haul himself up the branches in his tree. Chimpanzees are thoughtful beings and Eddie knew he was getting weaker. Without your generosity, Eddie, and others like him, will simply wither away. Abuse like this is a dreadful scar on our conscience. Text 'EDDIE' to our number for a £1 donation to support our programmes.

> Cared for in a dirty and small cage, Eddie was so weak and thin he could no longer climb up the branches in his tree. Chimpanzees are cunning beasts and Eddie knew he was getting weaker. Without your contribution, Eddie, and others like him, will simply get worse. Treatment like this is a bad thing that we should think about. Text 'EDDIE' to our number for a £1 donation that will go towards our programmes.

10 Look at the words/phrases below that are used in the leaflets. Draw three columns with the headings 'Negative', 'Neutral' and 'Positive'. Place each of the words/phrases in the column you think most appropriate.

thin   climb   haul up   generosity   beasts   abuse
contribution   scrawny   dirty   thoughtful   beings
squalid   cunning   treatment   support   donation

Combining different words in noun phrases can modify meaning and effect. This can be dramatic or quite subtle.

'Thoughtful beings'   adjective suggests intelligence, perhaps even kindness
noun 'beings' links to 'human beings' and to the idea of life being important

11 Annotate the phrase 'cunning beasts' in the same way.

12 Find other noun phrases in the two extracts and draw up a table like the one below, explaining their meaning and effect.

Noun phrase	Means	Effect
'thoughtful beings'	Intelligent life-forms	Makes the reader think of Eddie as more than an animal
'squalid and claustrophobic cage'	Dirty and suffocating place of imprisonment	Makes the reader think of Eddie being punished and driven mad by his surroundings

To save some money, your local zoo is planning to sell some of its animals to a zoo on the other side of the world. You object to this for the following reasons:

- The animals will need to be drugged to make them calm for the journey.

- They will travel many kilometres in cramped containers.

- The other zoo has had complaints of animal mistreatment.

- Photos suggest that animals are not fed properly at the destination zoo.

- Selling animals is not the only solution to the zoo's financial difficulties.

 13 Write a letter to the director of the zoo persuading him or her not to sell the animals.

How might this differ if you were arguing your case in a more balanced way?

> Some argue that sending animals to other zoos is a perfectly normal procedure and that the animals' comfort is paramount. However, others say that the effect of extended air travel is problematic, to say the least. And, at its worst, forcing animals to travel in suffocating containers for thousands of kilometres is utterly unacceptable.

- acknowledges another side to the argument
- positive words
- strong adjective in favour of this argument
- introduces contrasting viewpoint
- less intense word choice
- emotive noun phrase
- intensifier establishes strength of viewpoint

14 Read the example above, then write a second letter that presents both sides of the argument while still reaching a definite conclusion.

Checklist for success

- ✔ Make sure you present *both* sides of the argument.

- ✔ Use less emotive or intense vocabulary to begin with, but built sentences or paragraphs to a climax with increasingly powerful language.

Check your progress:

Sound progress 》》

I can select words and phrases according to their strength to reflect my views.

I can use balanced vocabulary to consider both sides of the argument.

Excellent progress 》》》

I can combine nouns, verbs, adjectives and adverbs to persuade the reader of my point of view.

I can move from balanced vocabulary to vivid and emotive word choices in each paragraph.

Use imperative and modal verbs to convey tone and levels of certainty

You will learn how to

- distinguish between the effects of imperative verbs and other verb forms
- select appropriate modal verbs to convey certainty or caution.

Different verb forms have different effects. When writing to argue or persuade, you can choose verb forms of different strengths to suit your purpose and your audience.

Getting you thinking

Read this letter to the managing director of a well-known mobile-phone company.

> Dear Mr Smart
>
> There are loads of dangers from mobile phones. They cause damage to eardrums and annoy people on trains when they are used for listening to music. Isn't it obvious? Fit all your phones with maximum volume controls. Act now!
>
> Yours,
>
> Iva Headache

1 Would this letter persuade Mr Smart? Why or why not? How could you make it more persuasive?

Imperative verbs are often used for commands or instructions. In the letter above, the imperative is *'Act* now!'

2 What effect does the imperative here have on the tone of the letter?

Exploring the skills

Modal verbs are auxiliary verbs that come at the front of the *verb chain*. Modals modify or alter the precise meaning of other verbs, and can be useful in persuasive writing.

Top tip

Modal verbs or expressions (can/could/may/might/must/shall/should/will/would/used to/ought to) express varying degrees of possibility, necessity or willingness to act. Some other expressions, such as 'appear to', 'seem to' and 'need to', also act like modals.

Read this longer letter sent by another campaigner.

Dear Mr Smart

I am writing to express my concern about the issues that might arise
from using mobile phones. I know that mobile phones could be considered
essential to everyday life, but it should be possible to do something
about their negative aspects. Mobile phones may damage eardrums if
used for listening to loud music. Also, while it might be enjoyable to listen
to music on a train, it can be annoying to hear the tinny beat right next to
you from someone else's phone.

You could perhaps fit your phones with lower maximum volume controls.
Also, you could work with train companies to publicise how irritating
headphone noise can be. These two steps will improve things immediately.

'might' in front of 'arise' suggests potential problem

'could' suggests not everyone sees them as 'essential'

'should' offers an expectation and strengthens the argument

'will' strengthens the argument and adds certainty

3 Look at the modals highlighted, then list any others you can find.

✐ Write a short paragraph explaining how the *tone* of this letter is different
from the first. Consider how persuasive it is and whether the choice of
nouns or adjectives alters the tone.

Developing the skills

5 What is the difference in meaning between these sentences?

> He might go to the doctor about that problem
> caused by his mobile phone.

> He ought to go to the doctor about that problem
> caused by his mobile phone.

> **Top tip**
>
> Remember, modals can
> temper or strengthen
> arguments. In a phrase
> like 'You must go',
> 'must' modifies 'go' and
> *strengthens* what is said.

Applying the skills

✐ Write an email to a mobile-phone manufacturer arguing for
some changes to the design or features of a mobile phone.
Use modal verbs.

Check your progress:

Checklist for success

Sound progress ⟫⟫

I can use some modal verbs in
a persuasive email.

✔ Choose modals carefully: you want to argue convincingly,
but you must not alienate the reader.

Excellent progress ⟫⟫⟫

✔ Use any other techniques you have learned, such as well-
selected noun phrases and adverbs, to argue your case.

I can use a wide range of
modal verbs to control the
tone of my email.

Use conjunctions and conjunctive adverbs to write coherent arguments

You will learn how to

- develop or contrast ideas in persuasive and argument texts using conjunctions and conjunctive adverbs.

You need to structure paragraphs using a range of cohesive devices in order to present arguments and counter-arguments clearly, and to develop and expand on a point of view.

Glossary

conjunction: a word used to join clauses or words in the same clause or sentence – for example 'and', 'but', 'or'

Getting you thinking

When you write to explore ideas or issues, try to use different types of connecting words and phrases.

Read the example below.

> Tidal energy is plentiful and can generate significant power.

— first idea
— second idea
— conjunction gives additional or equivalent information to support the first idea

Now look at this second example.

> Tidal energy is plentiful, yet it can be difficult to harness.

 1   Which is the **conjunction** in the second example? What is its function? (Is it supporting the first idea or doing something else?)

Exploring the skills

2   You can use conjunctions for different purposes. Match each conjunction to its purpose.

Conjunction	Purpose
Idea + *and* + idea	To offer an alternative
Idea + *so* + idea	To give additional information
Idea + *but* + idea	To give a reason
Idea + *or* + idea	To show a result or consequence
Idea + *because* + idea	To give a contrast, or indicate a difference or problem

Some adverbs connect ideas or actions across different sentences to suggest causes and sequences through a text. These **conjunctive adverbs** include words or phrases such as 'however', 'finally' and 'immediately'.

 What is the purpose of each conjunction or conjunctive adverb in the passage below?

Tidal energy is plentiful, yet can be difficult to harness. We need to invest in research in order to find out how practical it is. However, this is not straight forward as research costs a lot of money.

— conjunction
— conjunction
— conjunctive adverb
— conjunction

Constructing paragraphs that use conjunctions or conjunctive adverbs to build arguments is a key skill. Look at how it is done in this opening to a speech made by a student about wind turbines.

Every train journey or drive along a major route or road in the UK now reveals a wonderful phenomenon – wind turbines. These inspiring structures, sprouting like giants from the landscape, are huge and beautiful. They attract the eye like wonderful visitors from another planet. People even divert their journeys in order to experience the thrill of seeing them up close. Indeed, I love them because of their other-worldly appearance, and, furthermore, I'd be happy to have one of them stand guard over my own house. **2**

Glossary

conjunctive adverb: an adverb that links independent clauses in a sentence, or links ideas between two sentences – for example, 'finally', 'therefore', 'moreover' – to show cause and effect

1 Topic sentence introduces the subject of the speech.

2 Follow-up sentences give supporting detail to the argument about wind turbines.

4 What is the *viewpoint* expressed here? How do we know this from the very first sentence?

5 Make a note of any examples of conjunctions or adverbs used to

a) add further information or evidence (that is, one idea plus another one)

b) strengthen an idea

c) present the outcome or consequence of something.

6 Note down any other language devices that support the argument (for example, the choice of adjectives or noun phrases).

7 Write an opening paragraph in the same vein, but this time arguing *against* wind turbines. Make sure you use conjunctions or conjunctive adverbs to add information or strengthen ideas, and to show the outcome of a course of action.

You could start:

> Every train journey or drive along a major route or road in the UK now reveals a dreadful spectacle – wind turbines. These...

Top tip

Don't forget the important role pronouns and determiners can play in binding paragraphs together. For example, 'them' or 'these' refer back to the objects that have just been mentioned.

Developing the skills

In a text where you want to present points in a straightforward way, you might use conjunctive adverbs such as 'Firstly', 'Secondly' and 'Finally' to sequence ideas. However, you need to take a different approach if you want to weigh up or contrast those ideas or arguments.

Read this text from *Country Life* magazine. Think about how it sets up the debate and then introduces the different arguments for and against fracking.

Hailed as a game changer and the harbinger of cheap energy or as an ecological disaster, the cause of earthquakes and pollution, fracking's entrance into our lives has been colourful. The fundamentals are clear. Fracking is a method of extracting gas from rock formations by using high-pressure water and chemicals.

It enables us to extract from places that were hitherto uneconomic, but it's not cheap and is only cost-effective because of the high price of energy. Nevertheless, in the USA, it has transformed costs and is rapidly replacing coal as a source of generation. Dirty coal produces higher emissions, so fracked gas cuts American pollution and allows the country to claim to be fighting climate change. However, gas, like coal, is a fossil fuel. Its emissions are significant and, in the absence of carbon capture and storage, still contribute hugely to global warming.

'Fracking: the pros and cons', Lord Deben and Emma Hughes, *Country Life* magazine website

8 According to the article, what are the arguments for and against fracking?

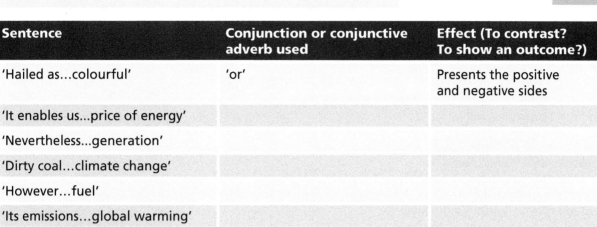

9 How are the different ideas presented? Copy and complete this table to track the progress of the debate.

Sentence	Conjunction or conjunctive adverb used	Effect (To contrast? To show an outcome?)
'Hailed as...colourful'	'or'	Presents the positive and negative sides
'It enables us...price of energy'		
'Nevertheless...generation'		
'Dirty coal...climate change'		
'However...fuel'		
'Its emissions...global warming'		

Applying the skills

10 You have learned that a wind farm is to be built very close to your village or town. The council has invited people to come to a public meeting to express their views and you have asked to make a speech arguing against wind turbines. Write your speech. Here are some potential arguments you could include:

- spoils natural beauty of landscape
- costs too much: currently wind energy not as efficient as fossil fuel or nuclear energy; farms are expensive to build
- noise pollution: some people living close to turbines claim low-level noise causes stress-related illness
- can disrupt TV and radio signals
- affects migration of birds when not positioned correctly
- Ministry of Defence worried that offshore wind farms could interfere with coastal radar systems.

Checklist for success

✔ Begin with a paragraph that sets up the argument (look again at the 'pro-turbine' example in Activity 4).

✔ Link ideas in your paragraphs by using the conjunctions and conjunctive adverbs you have come across in this unit. Here are some others you could use: *in order that, since, unless, until, whenever, while, similarly, likewise, nonetheless, furthermore, accordingly, otherwise, in fact.*

✔ Use these conjunctions or conjunctive adverbs to give reasons, strengthen points, suggest outcomes or present the other side of the case in order to knock it down.

Check your progress:
....

Sound progress 》》
I can write a sequence of paragraphs that clearly sets out my argument against wind turbines.

Excellent progress 》》》
I can set out my argument clearly and move fluently between points within the paragraphs by using conjunctions and conjunctive adverbs.

Vary word and clause order in sentences to create particular effects

You will learn how to

- order words and clauses in sentences to encourage different responses from your reader.

You can vary the word order in sentences to **foreground** certain ideas in order to persuade your reader of a particular viewpoint.

Glossary

foreground: to bring to the front or bring to attention

Getting you thinking

An advertising executive wants to use a comment from a food expert to highlight the merits of a particular brand of chocolate. Here are three choices for the advert.

> Food expert says chocolate's good for you.
>
> Chocolate's good for you, says food expert.
>
> Chocolate's good for you.

1 What is different about each of these versions? Look at word order and what has been left in or omitted.

What difference is there in the meaning or effect?

Exploring the skills

In an argument or persuasive text, it might seem natural to foreground the main clause by positioning it at the start of a sentence.

Children are suffering from increased numbers of dental problems, **1** because they are drinking very sugary juice from concentrate. **2**

1 Main clause draws attention to the general idea, 'dental problems'.

2 Subordinate clause placed second makes the reason – 'juice from concentrate' – of secondary importance.

3 What would be the effect of changing around the clause order of this sentence?

You can usually change the order of a complex sentence with a subordinate clause that hinges on a subordinating conjunction such as 'because', 'even after', 'although' and 'notwithstanding'.

 Add a different conjunction to the sentences below. Then rewrite them, changing the clause order. Do they still work?

a) _____ torrential rain was falling, we decided to carry on with the match.

b) She raced onto the platform _____ the guard had told her the train had left.

Developing the skills

You can also use the order of clauses in sentences to anticipate counter-arguments when pushing your own viewpoint.

Many people claim that juice from concentrate is better for their children than fizzy drinks , but experts have reported that in many cases such juices actually have a higher percentage of sugars.

 Counter-argument placed at start of sentence.

 'but' is the hinge word that signals the 'answer' to the counter-argument.

5 What do you think the viewpoint of the writer is? What point is being rebutted by the 'experts'?

6 How else does the writer suggest that the counter-argument is false?

Now read this related article.

Recent research claims that chocolate can have hidden health benefits, but are these claims true? It may be the case that the caffeine in chocolate can make you feel more alert, but the large amount of sugar means there's a heavy price to pay in terms of weight gain and tooth decay. Even if very dark chocolate does contain some antioxidants, which may prevent heart disease, the truth is that very few young people like these non-sugary varieties of chocolate. Instead they prefer sweeter types that do not contain such chemicals.

7 Identify two occasions where anticipated counter-arguments are placed in the first clause of a sentence.

Applying the skills

8 Write the front page of a health leaflet arguing that you should try to avoid buying fruit juices from concentrate and instead either buy pure-pressed juices or drink alternatives. Include arguments about preservatives, the five-a-day fruit content and the taste. Mention the merits of water.

Checklist for success

✔ Foreground counter-arguments so you can rebut them in the second part of your sentences.

✔ Think about using simple statements to introduce paragraphs, followed by a few related ideas.

Top tip

For a leaflet, use a combination of short, concise text (titles, headings or bulleted lists) and longer explanations. Think about how a three- or four-word heading for the leaflet could capture readers' attention.

Check your progress:

Sound progress 〉〉〉
I can change word order in a sentence in my leaflet so that some words stand out.

Excellent progress 〉〉〉
I can vary the word and clause order of sentences in a leaflet to guide the reader's response.

Vary sentence types to persuade readers

You will learn how to

- select a range of sentence types for different effects when persuading others.

Using different lengths and styles of sentence can help you appeal to readers' emotions or get across your viewpoint in a piece of writing.

Getting you thinking

You see the notice on the right on a board at your school.

1 Would this notice persuade you to participate in the race or to find out more about it? What is good or bad about the text?

> There is a charity fun race that is happening. It is to support local children living on the street. I want to make a difference to their lives which are terrible. They don't even have a warm bed to sleep in or a family. You can contact me if you want to help. I am in Class 1OA and my name is Ruth.

Exploring the skills

Now look at this page from a website.

website name/title   main motto   subheading   explanation   request/command

2 a) Judging from the text and images, what is the main purpose of this website? How long did it take you to work this out?

b) What is the purpose of each section of text highlighted?

c) Are all the sentences the same type?

3 Copy and complete the table below.

Text examples	Sentence features (i.e. question, tense, type of verbs used)	Effect
'Fighting for street children'	**Minor sentence** Uses present participle '-ing'	Easy to remember, like a motto Suggests an ongoing battle – not giving up
'Could you spare your time too?'	Question Possessive 'your'	
'Their time is making a difference.'		
'Railway Children volunteers are helping to change the lives of vulnerable children living alone and at risk on the streets.'		

Developing the skills

By using a variety of sentence types you can

- make your reader take notice – for example, with short, succinct sentences or **minor sentences**

- make a direct appeal by addressing readers in the second person (using pronouns such as 'you', 'we' or possessives like 'yours', 'our')

- show your evidence or reasoning through longer explanations that follow or precede shorter, more direct statements

- encourage action by using the imperative where appropriate.

4 Copy the text on the right and annotate it to show how it demonstrates all the features listed above.

Applying the skills

5 Sketch a basic one-page website design for a charity you and your classmates have set up called 'Street Smart', which helps children who are living on the street. Write about 100 words on the home page to persuade other students to join the campaign.

Checklist for success

- ✔ Design your web page with different areas, including a motto, heading and links.

- ✔ Use a range of sentence types and lengths.

- ✔ Consider aspects such as tenses and direct address.

Glossary

minor sentence: expressions that do not contain a complete verb, but which are still regarded as sentences ('Bikes for hire!', 'No thanks!'). They may not have a full stop, as they are often used as headings or mottos.

Want to help others? Tick. Want to do something useful with your life? Tick. Want to make a difference? Tick. If you join our campaign to help young people get their lives back on track, then you'll be ticking all those boxes. Give us a call now.

Check your progress:

Sound progress ⟫⟫

I can use short and long sentences, as well as some simple, direct headings on a website page.

Excellent progress ⟫⟫⟫

I can use a wide range of sentence types and styles to create a varied and impactful web page.

Select punctuation to convey your opinions appropriately

You will learn how to

- select punctuation appropriately to fit the tone and purpose of your writing
- use rhetorical questions and semicolons in argument pieces.

Punctuation can help you get your viewpoint across and organise your arguments effectively.

Getting you thinking

Read this email sent to the manager of a large multiplex cinema.

> **To: Manager, BigChain Cinemas**
> **From: L. Smith**
> I'm emailing you about an important issue to me as a regular cinema-goer. Popcorn! I'm fed up with it! It really irritates me and my friends! Every time we go someone ruins our night with their noisy eating! Couldn't you ban it for one night a week? Here's why. You wouldn't lose much money! You'd gain more customers like us! There'd be less cleaning up!
> Thanks!
> Lucy Smith

> What is the effect of using so many exclamation marks here? How does it make the writer sound?

Exploring the skills

Now look at this second example.

> **To: Manager, BigChain Cinemas**
> **From: M. King**
> I'm emailing you about an important issue to me as a regular cinema-goer – popcorn. I'm fed up with it. It really irritates me and my friends; every time we go someone ruins our night with their noisy eating. Couldn't you ban it for one night a week? Here's why: you wouldn't lose much money, you'd gain more customers like us, and there'd be less cleaning up.
> Yours,
> Max King

> The removal of the exclamation mark and the creation of a single sentence with a dash in it makes the word 'popcorn' simply the explanation of what the issue is.
>
> What other changes have been made to the punctuation in this email and what is the effect of each change?

3 How you would describe the tone in the second version? (Informal? Aggressive? Reasonable? Well-argued? Angry? Spiteful?)

4 Which of the two emails is more likely to be successful? Why?

Now read this new extract, which comes from an opinion piece in a national paper.

> The problem with watching a film with other people is... other people! There are so many things I dislike about them: they're disgusting, noisy and (let's be honest here) stupid. Isn't it the height of ignorance to talk on their mobiles when they've paid to watch the film?

1 Ellipsis delays the punch-line, perhaps making you think something else is going to be said.

2 Brackets allow the writer to make an 'aside', as if he or she is taking you into their confidence.

5 Write short answers to these questions.

   a) There is just one use of an exclamation mark here. How does it add to the effect of the first sentence?

   b) How does the colon in the second sentence help with developing the argument?

The writer uses a **rhetorical question** to end the article. Rhetorical questions are often used to add weight or power to an argument.

6 How does the rhetorical question in this case add to or support what was said in the previous sentence?

Glossary

rhetorical question:
a question that does not require an answer, or which answers itself

Developing the skills

Now read this longer opinion piece about modern cinemas.

> See, the thing is, I hate popcorn. Not the taste or the substance of the foodstuff itself, which is every bit as yummy and nutritious as exploded mushroom clouds of super-heated dried grain smothered in salt and/or sugar plus a cocktail of super-poisonous chemicals (Google 'pop-corn' and 'chemicals' and check it out – you'll be shocked) and packed in cardboard can possibly be. As a child I used to surreptitiously chew those Styrofoam worms in which fragile electrical appliances are packed for shipping, and taste-wise there wasn't a whole lot of difference between them and the buttered delights now sold in vast quantities in cinema foyers around the world. Certainly the overall effect was the same: much munching, zero nourishment and an overpowering need to quench your thirst with whichever carbonated brand of tooth-napalm came most easily to hand. To my mind, popcorn has always been a bit like heroin: the first hit makes you want to throw up (apparently), but also leaves you with a craving to quell the nausea by ingesting industrial amounts of the very thing which made you sick in the first place. Cigarettes are the same – or so smokers tell me – ghastly, but in a moreish kind of way.
>
> **Mark Kermode, *The Good, the Bad and the Multiplex***

Mark Kermode uses a range of punctuation to help express and argue his viewpoint. Copy and complete this table.

Punctuation feature	Where used	Purpose	Effect
Brackets	(Google...shocked)	To provide supporting evidence	Adds factual impact to the argument
Brackets	(apparently)		
Colon			
Colon			
Dash			
Dash			

How would you describe Kermode's style? What is his viewpoint?

It is important not to get so obsessed with looking at one language element (such as punctuation) that you ignore other, equally important, aspects of a writer's techniques. Mark Kermode uses many persuasive techniques in his text.

9 Find each of the following techniques in the extract by Mark Kermode, then write down why they have been used and what effect each one has:

a) a variety of short and long sentences

b) a personal anecdote

c) **hyperbole** in the form of exaggerated imagery or descriptive noun phrases

d) informal turns of phrase or **ellipsis**.

One technique Kermode does *not* employ in his article is the semicolon. However, in this alternative article about popcorn, the writer uses it on two occasions.

> We should not get rid of popcorn; we should keep it because of its taste, its financial help to cinemas, and – most important of all – its history. Popcorn takes us back in time; it transports us to the golden age of Hollywood.

10 What is the function of the semicolons here?

Glossary

hyperbole: exaggerated language or ideas often used to praise or criticise someone or something

ellipsis: the omission of a word or words that you can work out from the remaining parts of the phrase or sentence (for example, 'See' really means, 'You see')

11 Write an opinion piece for a magazine for people aged 16 to 24, in which you argue that going to music festivals is a very unpleasant experience and is best avoided. Your tone should be slightly comic, like Mark Kermode's, but you should make some truthful points.

Include comments on

- facilities
- weather
- other festival goers
- transport
- the bands
- prices
- friends you go with.

Checklist for success

- ✔ Use punctuation carefully and don't over-use one particular type, such as exclamation marks or brackets.
- ✔ Consider how colons or semicolons can help develop an argument or set of points.
- ✔ Judge your audience and the tone you need – how chatty can it be?
- ✔ Consider anything else you have learned about effective persuasion or argument.

Check your progress:

Sound progress ⟫

I can choose punctuation accurately to write a comic opinion piece without over-using one type of punctuation.

Excellent progress ⟫⟫

I can select a range of punctuation to establish a comic tone while accurately expressing my viewpoint.

Structure argument and persuasive texts effectively

You will learn how to

- organise paragraphs in different ways for different effects.

The order or arrangement of your ideas throughout a text can have a big impact on how a reader will respond to your argument.

Getting you thinking

There are several ways to organise argument or persuasive texts. The table below covers one or two points per paragraph.

Paragraph	Structure 1	Structure 2	Structure 3
Introduction	General overview of issue	General overview of issue	General overview of issue
1	Points 1–2 for topic	Points 1–2 for topic	Point 1 for and against
2	Points 3–4 for topic	Points 1–2 against topic	Point 2 for and against
3	Point 5 for topic	Points 3–4 for topic	Point 3 for and against
4	Points 1–2 against topic	Points 3–4 against topic	Point 4 for and against
5	Points 3–4 against topic	Point 5 for topic	Point 5 for and against
6	Point 5 against topic	Point 5 against topic	
Conclusion	Your view – for or against and why	Your view – for or against and why	Your view – for or against and why

1 Which structure do you think would be the easiest to plan for and to write? Why?

What reasons might there be not to choose this approach?

> **Top tip**
>
> A good argument text is not just about being clear, but also about sustaining your viewpoint and engaging your reader throughout.

Exploring the skills

Here is a short paragraph from an article about whether horse-racing should be banned.

> Many people argue that horse-racing is the sport of kings and has a long and noble history that goes back centuries to the time of chivalry and honour. However, it is difficult to support this view when there have been so many recent scandals to do with cheating and doping.

Which of the three structures does this paragraph use, Structure 1, 2 or 3?

Developing the skills

There are two main benefits to considering one 'for' and one 'against' argument in each paragraph.

- It makes your writing more interesting, because you are expressing your view throughout rather than just listing points for and then points against.

- It allows you to deal with the counter-argument against your chosen point, and knock it down.

When using this structure, you need to make sure there are points for and against that naturally go together.

Top tip

Conjunctions and conjunctive adverbs will be vital for the success of your structure. See page 55 for some examples you could use.

 4 Look at the table below and link the arguments for and against horse-racing. One example has been done for you.

For	Against
1 Racehorses are treated well by their owners and looked after in comfort.	**a** Horse-racing has recently had scandals to do with doping and cheating.
2 Racing is a big business and provides work for jockeys, trainers, stable-hands and people at racecourses.	**b** Horses can be mistreated in training and racing through the use of the whip to make them run faster.
3 Horse-racing is an ancient, noble sport that goes back centuries.	**c** Much of the money comes from betting and encouraging people to bet money can lead to addiction to gambling.
4 Horses are cared for before and after races, with vets on hand should there be accidents.	**d** Most races are very boring – and they last only a few minutes.
5 Horse-racing is an exciting and enjoyable spectacle showcasing real skills.	**e** Every year, horses die while racing, either from bad falls or heart attacks caused by over-exertion.

Applying the skills

5 Draft an article for or against horse-racing. Decide on your structure before you begin. It will show more skill to an examiner if you can consider the points for and against in one paragraph, or move from points for in one paragraph to points against in the next.

Checklist for success

- ✔ Plan your article before you begin writing.

- ✔ Choose your structure and stick to it all the way through.

- ✔ Make sure you provide arguments both for and against before reaching your conclusion.

Check your progress:

Sound progress 〉〉〉

I can make my views on horse-racing clear, using points for and against in well-structured paragraphs.

Excellent progress 〉〉〉

I can link points for and against horse-racing within paragraphs, using the structure of the essay to explore counter-arguments.

Check your progress

Sound progress 》》》

- ☐ I can select and use nouns, adjectives, verbs and adverbs according to their strength to express my opinion.
- ☐ I can use choose my vocabulary to reflect both sides of an argument.
- ☐ I can use some modal verbs in a persuasive writing to adapt the tone of my argument.
- ☐ I can set out my argument coherently through a clear sequence of paragraphs.
- ☐ I can change the word order in my sentences so that some words and ideas stand out.
- ☐ I can use short and long sentences, as well as some simple, direct headings to get my message across.
- ☐ I can use punctuation accurately to convey my viewpoint.
- ☐ I can organise my paragraphs to make my viewpoint clear.

Excellent progress 》》》》

- ☐ I can combine nouns, adjectives, verbs and adverbs to persuade the reader of my point of view.
- ☐ I can vary my vocabulary from balanced word choices to the deliberate use of vivid and emotive words to express my viewpoint persuasively.
- ☐ I can use a wide range of modal verbs to control the tone of my writing.
- ☐ I can develop and contrast ideas fluently in an argument text using conjunctions and conjunctive adverbs.
- ☐ I can order words and clauses in sentences to encourage different responses from my reader.
- ☐ I can use a wide range of sentence types and styles to create persuasive texts with impact.
- ☐ I can use a wide range of punctuation, selecting each usage for deliberate effect on the reader.
- ☐ I can link points within paragraphs in persuasive texts, using structure to explore and rebuff counter-arguments.

Chapter 4
Writing to analyse, explore and comment

What's it all about?

When analysing other people's writing, it is important to pay attention to your own use of language. Writing clearly and precisely will enable your reader to follow your points easily.

This chapter will show you how to

- choose effective vocabulary for analytical writing
- choose sentence structures for clear analysis
- structure sentences to compare and contrast
- quote and explain writers' ideas effectively
- comment on writers' choices.

You will write

- an analysis of an opinion piece about tattoos
- an explanation of how a writer presents ideas about teenagers
- a comparison of two poems
- an analysis of a poem about anger
- a comment on a writer's use of language in an opinion article on the British summer.

Choose effective vocabulary for analytical writing

You will learn how to

- select effective verbs to discuss writers' choices
- select appropriate and specific adjectives and adverbs to characterise a writer's views.

Precise vocabulary choices help you make clear and detailed comments when you are analysing texts.

Getting you thinking

Here is an opinion article.

Tattoos are everywhere. You see them on firm young flesh and on wobbly, middle-aged flab, as common now on the school run and in the supermarket queue as they are on some footballer or his wife.

I feel like the last man left alive whose skin crawls at the sight of these crass daubings.

I feel like the *only* person in the world who sees David Beckham modelling his swimming pants on the cover of *Elle* magazine and thinks – oh, how much better a handsome guy like you would look, David, without all those dumb ink stains stitched into your skin.

I feel like nobody else looks at little Cheryl Cole – so pretty, so smiley – and recoils at the sight of the florist shop she has permanently engraved on her lovely body.

Tony Parsons, 'Making my skin crawl: tattoos screaming for attention', *The Daily Mirror,* **23 June 2012**

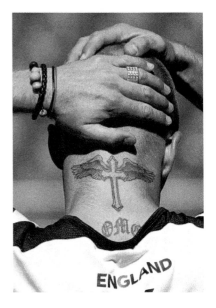

 1 What are Tony Parsons's views about tattoos and how does he present these views to the reader? Note down five words, phrases or language features that stand out to you.

Exploring the skills

When analysing texts, you need to explain how the writer uses certain language features to affect the reader. For example, Parsons's repeated pattern of 'I feel like the last man left alive/ the only person in the world/nobody else' makes us focus on how Parsons feels. It also emphasises how he believes that no one shares his views.

 2 For each of the five words, phrases or language features you noted in Activity 1, write down the effect it has.

Now turn three of your ideas into full sentences, analysing the effect of Parsons's language. Use a different verb in each sentence. You can choose from the verbs below, or think of your own.

describes	states	indicates	explores (how)	sets out (his ideas)
conveys	suggests	presents	emphasises	implies

Developing the skills

Summarising a writer's approach in an introductory sentence before commenting on specific language choices is a good way to provide an overview. Adjectives and adverbs are useful to help you sum up the overall effect.

Look at the vocabulary bank below. Select three adjectives and three adverbs that you could use when commenting on Parsons's text. You may be able to combine them (for example, 'deeply critical').

Adjectives	Adverbs
critical	relentlessly
judgemental	consistently
harsh	deeply
damning	uncompromisingly
disapproving	insistently
condemnatory	mercilessly
unforgiving	intensely
disparaging	acutely
censorious	severely

Applying the skills

5 Re-read the extract. Then write a full response to the question: 'What are Tony Parsons's views about tattoos and how does he present these views to the reader?'

Checklist for success

✔ Make sure that you choose adjectives and adverbs precisely to summarise Parsons's views.

✔ Use a variety of verbs in your analysis.

4.1

Top tip

When analysing a text, avoid describing everything as simply 'positive' or 'negative' – use a variety of words to describe the writer's viewpoint and quotations to back up your points.

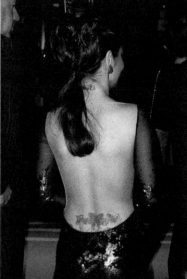

Check your progress:

Sound progress

I can choose a variety of verbs to discuss Parsons's ideas.

I can use adjectives and adverbs to analyse the language Parsons uses.

Excellent progress

I can discuss Parsons's views both in overview and in detail.

I can select and combine adjectives and adverbs to characterise Parsons's views clearly.

Choose sentence structures for clear analysis

You will learn how to

- construct sentences clearly to explain the effects of writers' choices
- use a range of subordinate clauses to add detail to analytical points.

Careful, conscious use of different sentence structures can help make your analysis of a writer's language use clear to the reader.

Getting you thinking

Read the text below.

Young people who arrive at sunshine destinations are unable to drag themselves away from their screens and spend hours each day on social networking sites like Facebook and Twitter.

On a typical 10-day holiday, teenagers are glued to smart phones, laptops or tablets for nearly 20 hours.

Facebook and texting are among the most popular activities, but one in 10 like to upload holiday pictures to Instagram and 40 per cent are hooked on online games.

A third of parents said their children barely look up from their smart phone while on holiday, and half of parents surveyed "despair" about the amount of time their children spend clutching gadgets when they're on a family holiday.

'Teenagers spend two hours a day social networking while on holiday', Olivia Goldhill, *Daily Telegraph*, 12 August 2013

'Explain how the writer presents her ideas about teenagers' holiday behaviour in this article.'

Note down three quotations and/or language features that you could explore when answering the question.

Exploring the skills

In explaining the effect of writers' choices on you as a reader, you should use sentences in a range of ways, considering

- what comes first in your sentence
- how you show logic and reasoning
- how to add detail.

Choose one of your quotations and construct it into a full sentence.

For example, for the quotation 'clutching gadgets', you might write:

> The writer **1** describes teenagers as 'clutching gadgets' in order to imply that teenagers rely too heavily on their gadgets, **2** as 'clutching' suggests desperation. **3**

1	Emphasises the writer's choices.
2	Conjunction (linking word) indicates an explanation will follow.
3	Clause of reason adds detail.

Developing the skills

You can structure analytical sentences in different ways for different effects.

Structure	Example	Effect
Subordinate clause of reason first	Because 'clutching' suggests desperation, the phrase 'clutching gadgets' implies that teenagers rely too heavily on their electronic devices.	Focuses on a specific effect and moves to a broader point
Start with quotation	'Clutching gadgets' is an effective way to imply that teenagers rely on their gadgets, as 'clutching' suggests desperation.	Highlights the quotation
Noun phrase introducing the general focus	Teenagers are portrayed as overly reliant on their gadgets, through the phrase 'clutching gadgets', as 'clutching' suggests desperation.	Emphasises the subject or topic
Noun phrase describing the effect of the quotation	An effective way to convey teenagers' reliance on their gadgets is shown in the phrase 'clutching gadgets', as 'clutching' suggests desperation.	Shows evaluation
Relative clause	The phrase 'clutching gadgets', which implies desperation, portrays teenagers as overly reliant on their gadgets.	Concisely shows a specific effect as part of a broader one

3 Produce three different versions of your sentence, following three of these patterns. What does each version help you to achieve?

Check your progress:

Applying the skills

4 Write a full answer to the practice question: 'Explain how the writer presents her ideas about teenagers' holiday behaviour in this article.'

Checklist for success

✔ Use the three points you originally identified and analyse them in detail.

✔ Make sure you start your sentences in different ways.

Sound progress ⟫⟫

I can start sentences in three different ways.

I can use sentence structure to draw the reader's attention to my points.

Excellent progress ⟫⟫

I can use subordinate clauses to vary the detail in my analysis of the article.

I can choose sentence structures to create a clear analysis of the writer's ideas.

Structure sentences to compare and contrast

You will learn how to

- select effective conjunctions, adverbs and punctuation to support comparison
- use comparative forms effectively.

In GCSE analysis, you will be asked to compare (to highlight and discuss similarities) and to contrast (to point out and explore differences). Some simple language tools can help you make clear and effective comparisons.

Getting you thinking

1 Look at the two poems below. Think about similarities and differences between them for two minutes. Use at least four of the following words to help you.

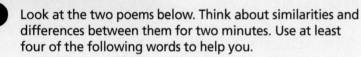

| both | equally | each | similarly |
| however | although | too | whereas |

'Nurse's Song' from *Songs of Innocence*

When the voices of children are heard
    on the green
And laughing is heard on the hill,
My heart is at rest within my breast
And everything else is still.

'Then come home my children; the sun is
    gone down
And the dews of night arise.
Come, come, leave off play and let us away,
Till the morning appears in the skies.'

'No, no, let us play, for it is yet day
And we cannot go to sleep.
Besides, in the sky the little birds fly,
And the hills are all covered with sheep.'

'Well, well go and play till the light fades away,
And then go home to bed.'
The little ones leaped and shouted and
    laughed
And all the hills echoèd.

William Blake

'Nurse's Song' from *Songs of Experience*

When the voices of children are heard on
    the green,
And whisperings are in the dale,
The days of my youth rise fresh in my
    mind,
My face turns green and pale.

Then come home my children, the sun is
    gone down,
And the dews of night arise.
Your spring and your day are wasted in
    play,
And your winter and night in disguise.

William Blake

Exploring the skills

Look at this paragraph comparing the presentation of the two nurses in the poems.

> Both poems show the nurses' feelings for the children in their care. The nurse from *Songs of Innocence* is presented as loving the children. We can see that she finds the children's laughter calming through the statement 'My heart is at rest'. The nurse in *Songs of Experience* seems to be suspicious of the children. She refers to 'whisperings', which makes them sound devious.

2 How successful is this paragraph as a comparison? Does it *link* or *contrast* the ideas sufficiently?

Signposting helps your reader follow your argument. You can use *adverbs* or *adverbials*, *conjunctions* and *determiners* to help you achieve this.

	For comparison	**For contrast**
Adverbs and *adverbials* (used at the start of a sentence or clause)	equally similarly in the same way likewise also	however on the other hand alternatively conversely
Conjunctions (link clauses within sentences)	and or	but whereas while although yet
Determiners	both each either neither	this that one the other

Top tip

Using an adverb or adverbial phrase at (or near) the start of a sentence lets the reader know that you are linking this sentence to what has gone before.

Look at the three sets of sentences below.

> The *Innocence* nurse shows a loving attitude towards the children. The *Experience* nurse seems to be more judgmental.

> The nurses respond to hearing the children's voices. They do this in different ways. The nurse in the first poem finds it reassuring. The nurse in the second poem seems to feel threatened by it.

> The poems have a natural and everyday feel. This may be because they do not use similes to describe the children.

3 Add adverbs/adverbials, conjunctions and determiners to combine sentences and make the links between the ideas more obvious. Then make any other minor changes so that the full analysis makes sense.

Developing the skills

Vocabulary choices are one way to make clear comparisons, but the way you structure your sentences can also help you to achieve this.

You can use a *semicolon* to show that points are strongly linked and to set up a clear contrast.

> Hearing the children makes the *Innocence* nurse feel calm; in contrast it makes the *Experience* nurse feel ill.

You can also use comparative forms of adjectives and adverbs to make links between texts. This is a good way of **evaluating** and commenting on specific aspects of texts.

There are three main types of comparative forms.

Form	Example
more/less... (than)	'Poem A uses a more complex rhyme scheme than Poem B.'
-er (than)	'X uses richer vocabulary than Y.'
as...as	'Text A is as formal as Text B in structure, but its vocabulary is more colloquial.'

4 Create three brief statements comparing the 'Nurse's Song' poems using the three forms above.

Top tip

Remember that semicolons connect *full main clauses*.

Glossary

evaluating: making judgements about effectiveness or quality

Comparatives are useful in presenting personal views, in which you weigh up the qualities of different texts.

> *The words chosen for emphasis through the rhyme scheme create, I feel, a more disturbing atmosphere in the Experience poem, particularly in the final stanza. While the Innocence poem rhymes 'arise' with 'the skies', Blake's selection of 'disguise' in the second version ends the poem on a sinister note.*

Another effective way to produce a detailed comparison is to move from a broad similarity to examine a more specific difference.

> *Although both articles present an individual's experience, Text A's use of personal pronouns creates a more intimate tone.*

 5 Select one of the comparisons you have already thought of and turn it into a broad/specific comparison following the pattern above.

Applying the skills

6 Compare the way Blake presents the nurses in his two 'Nurse's Song' poems.

Checklist for success

- ✔ Think about how you can use conjunctions, adverbs/adverbials and determiners to highlight your comparisons and contrasts to your reader.
- ✔ Make sure that you structure and link your sentences effectively to allow you to compare and contrast.
- ✔ Include comparative adjectives to comment on the poems' language.

Check your progress:

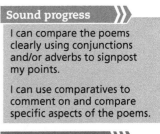

Sound progress

I can compare the poems clearly using conjunctions and/or adverbs to signpost my points.

I can use comparatives to comment on and compare specific aspects of the poems.

Excellent progress

I can use complex sentences to clearly compare and contrast the poems.

I can move confidently between broad comparisons and specific contrasts.

Quote and explain writers' ideas effectively

You will learn how to

- use quotation marks and other punctuation accurately when quoting
- embed and introduce quotations effectively.

Providing evidence for analytical points is crucial to making your arguments convincing. A key skill is being able to quote effectively.

Getting you thinking

1 Read the poem below, thinking about how the poet creates a sense of anger. Note down three main points of analysis with a quotation to illustrate each one.

Top tip

When a question asks you 'how' a writer does something, it is asking about the techniques and language used.

Anger Lay by Me

Anger lay by me all night long,
His breath was hot upon my brow,
He told me of my burning wrong,
All night he talked and would not go.

He stood by me all through the day,
Struck from my hand the book, the pen;
He said: 'Hear first what I've to say,
And sing, if you've the heart to, then.'

And can I cast him from my couch?
And can I lock him from my room?
Ah no, his honest words are such
That he's my true-lord, and my doom.

Elizabeth Daryush

Exploring the skills

Here are some of the key rules for quoting text.

Rule	Example
Quotation marks go around the quoted words.	The poet writes 'His breath was hot'.
Quotations should fit grammatically into the sentence.	The poet tells us that 'His breath was hot'.
Any quoted punctuation goes inside the quotation marks.	The speaker asks 'And can I cast him from my couch?'
Only quote what you need to – often a few words or even a single word is best.	The poet personifies anger as 'he'.

2 Which of the statements below do you think makes the best use of quotations?

> The poet personifies anger when she says, 'His breath was hot upon my brow, / He told me of my burning wrong, / All night he talked and would not go.'

> In the poem, anger is personified by 'he, his and him'.

> Personification is created in this poem. We know this because 'His breath'.

Developing the skills

3 Look back to your original points about the poem and write them out in full. Introduce your quotation in a different way each time.

It is important that your words and the words of the quotation fit together grammatically. You can do this by

- creating a relative clause using one of the relative pronouns: 'who', 'which' or 'that'
- changing the form of a quoted word using square brackets to show that you have done so.

Top tip

When quoting more than one line of verse, use a slanted line (/) to show line breaks.

Complete this table.

Sentence	Becomes...
Anger is described as 'lay by me all night long'	Anger is presented as a man who 'lay by me all night long
Anger is shown to be violent by 'Struck from my hand the book, the pen'	Anger is shown to be a violent force that...
The poet shows that she is powerless against anger as she doesn't know if 'can I cast him from my couch?'	

Applying the skills

Write an analysis of how the poet uses language to present anger. Think about techniques such as repetition and rhyme, as well as word choice and imagery.

Checklist for success

✔ Remember to use quotations to support your points.
✔ Punctuate your quotations accurately.
✔ Vary how you introduce embedded quotations.

Check your progress:

Sound progress »
I can choose suitable quotations from the poem.
I can embed the quotations accurately in my sentences.

Excellent progress »»
I can analyse the poem confidently using a range of quotations to support my points.
I can vary the way I embed the quotations in my clauses.

Comment on writers' choices

You will learn how to

- use paragraph openings carefully to create links within your writing
- use a range of paragraph structures in analysing texts.

Connecting paragraphs effectively to signal your overall argument to your reader is a useful way to improve your analytical writing.

Getting you thinking

Read this extract from an opinion column piece.

> Now the sun is finally shining, many of us have been reminded of how annoying it is. It makes you sweat and squint, it burns your skin, it renders a smartphone, left casually on a table top, too hot to send texts.
>
> A few years ago, I went to a barbecue on a May afternoon in London. We were 'lucky with the weather': the sun was shining. About a dozen of us, self-consciously grateful for the clear sky, sat awkwardly on the grass, pale and shiny, as the sunlight beat down – using one hand as an improvised peak or brim, because we'd forgotten to own hats, and the other to prop ourselves upright, because we'd forgotten to develop stomach muscles.
>
> **'The British summer would be far more tolerable without sunshine'**, David Mitchell, *The Observer*, 14 July 2013

Note down at least five words or phrases that you would comment on to answer the question: 'How does David Mitchell use language to present his views about the British summer?'

Exploring the skills

To use paragraphs effectively, you need to plan what you are going to say in each paragraph. The ideas you have should be summarised briefly in an introductory paragraph, then each idea should form the basis of a topic sentence for the main body paragraphs.

2 Create a simple plan for your answer, using some of the ideas you came up with in Activity 1.

Draft a short opening paragraph that introduces the main ideas for your reader.

Developing the skills

Look at this extract from a response to the question in Activity 1.

> The writer emphasises how annoying the sun is by making a list. Phrases such as 'burns your skin' and 'makes you sweat' are used to show how the sun affects us. This is effective because it reminds the reader of the worst things about the sun.
>
> The text uses adverbs to show how people in Britain react to the sunny weather. For example, it tells us that they were 'self-consciously grateful' and they sat 'awkwardly'. This is effective because it shows the negative ways in which people react.

4   Rewrite the second paragraph to introduce some variation (for example, by changing the order to avoid repetition).

Linking your paragraphs carefully can make your overall argument more fluent. Connectives such as 'firstly' and 'furthermore' can show connections.

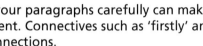 How many different ways of joining paragraphs can you think of to convey the meanings in the table below? One example is given for each.

> **Top tip**
>
> Using a range of sentence structures within paragraphs can also make your writing more varied.

Meaning	Example
Here's another similar idea or some more evidence.	Furthermore,
Here's a contrasting idea.	On the other hand,
I'm going back to a previous idea.	As mentioned earlier,
I know people have different views.	Although some people may claim that...
I'm bringing everything together.	In conclusion,

Applying the skills

Write a response to the question: 'How does David Mitchell use language to present his views about the British summer?'

Checklist for success

✔ Use a short introduction to give an overview of your points.

✔ Link your paragraphs together using joining words.

✔ Vary your paragraphs' structure.

Check your progress:

Sound progress »

I can write a concise introduction that sets out my overall argument.

I can make clear and easy-to-follow connections between my paragraphs.

Excellent progress »»

I can write an easy-to-follow argument throughout my answer.

My paragraph structures link in a sophisticated way.

Check your progress

Good progress »»

- [ ] I can use verbs effectively to analyse how writers communicate their ideas.
- [ ] I can use adjectives and adverbs effectively to analyse language.
- [ ] I can begin sentences with different subordinate clauses or noun phrases.
- [ ] I can use sentence structure to draw the reader's attention to the most relevant parts of my text.
- [ ] I can use conjunctions and/or adverbs to signpost my points when comparing texts.
- [ ] I can punctuate my quotations accurately.
- [ ] I can use embedded quotations in a way that fits the grammar of my own sentences.
- [ ] I can plan an analysis with an introduction and paragraphs built around a topic sentence.
- [ ] I can make clear links between my paragraphs.

Excellent progress »»»

- [ ] I can move from an overview to the detail of a text confidently, selecting the most relevant language features to analyse.
- [ ] I can use different types of subordinate clause to provide different kinds of detail when analysing a text.
- [ ] I can use a variety of paragraph structures to create fluent, articulate analysis.
- [ ] I can use sentence structure effectively in comparisons, including complex sentences and careful punctuation.
- [ ] I can use quotations confidently, using single words and lists of words/phrases as well as whole phrases or sentences when appropriate.
- [ ] I can vary the ways my quotations fit into my sentences, including relative pronouns to create embedded clauses.
- [ ] I can comment on writers' choices using a range of paragraph structures.
- [ ] I can link my paragraphs in a variety of ways.

Chapter 5
Writing to summarise

What's it all about?

Writing to summarise means being able to understand other texts and to draw out the key points and express them in your own words.

This chapter will show you how to

- summarise in your own words
- summarise effectively using complex sentences.

You will write

- a summary of an eye-witness account of the effects of a forest fire
- a summary of problems on the roads in India.

Summarise in your own words

You will learn how to

- use synonyms and collective nouns to paraphrase effectively.

Being able to summarise ideas is a useful skill for life and study, as it can help you make sense of information and put it into your own words.

Getting you thinking

Read these two short extracts relating to a news feature on the aftermath of a storm.

A

> As I made my way through the dense woods, I observed how pine, ash, oak and elm had all been scarred, snapped in half or uprooted by the violent weather.

B

> Going through the forest, the writer noted the storm-damaged trees.

 What is the connection between these two texts?

2 In what ways are they different? Which one is a summary text?

Exploring the skills

In order to summarise effectively, you need to be able to **paraphrase**. To do this you will need to use **synonyms**.

3 Find the synonyms in Text B for these words from Text A:

a) 'dense woods'

b) 'observed'.

The writer of Text B **synthesises** the specific words 'pine', 'ash', 'oak' and 'elm' under the single, more general term 'trees'.

 Which specific words in Text A have been replaced by the more general term 'storm-damaged'?

Read this further section from the same article on the effects of forest storms and fires.

> The future of local inhabitants is intimately connected to the forest. The life-giving fibrous roots, lichen and fruits from the trees nourish the soil and help deer and wild boar to flourish, ready for hunting. In the past, locals have

Glossary

paraphrase: to rewrite something in your own words

synonyms: words that are the same or similar in meaning

synthesises: combines separate elements or parts

managed the forest responsibly, taking only what they require, maintaining the ecosystem's delicate balance. But the fires have ruined all that. In addition, there is another problem. Rather than wait for the forest to regenerate, local people have understandably returned to intensive farming, bringing in cows, goats and sheep to graze on what was once woodland. Persuading local people to take the long-term view has proved futile.

Think of synonyms for the highlighted words.

Developing the skills

When you are summarising, you are trying to be concise. You can do this by

- using a collective noun to replace specific examples: 'family' is the collective noun you might use for 'brother, sister, mother, father'
- using determiners/pronouns such as 'they' and 'these' to avoid repetition.

6 Read the text again.

a) What words could the general term 'nutrients' replace in the text?

b) What collective nouns could you use instead of 'cows, goats and sheep' and 'deer and wild boar'.

Which phrase towards the end of the text could you replace with the pronoun 'them'?

Applying the skills

8 Re-read the longer extract about the forest. Note down

a) key points about local people's relationship to the forest before the fires

b) key points about how this relationship changed after the fires.

Sum up these ideas in 50–55 words.

Checklist for success

✔ Leave out information out that isn't needed or that is repeated, using pronouns or other techniques.

✔ Use synonyms or collective nouns for key words or phrases.

✔ Use your own words where possible.

Top tip

Sometimes you can use **antonyms** if you can't think of synonyms: for example, 'not impossible' is similar in meaning to 'possible'.

Glossary

antonyms: words or phrases that are opposite in meaning

Top tip

Concision is also about leaving out the less important details. When writing to summarise, consider whether a piece of information is relevant to the task, or whether you could omit it.

Check your progress:

Sound progress »»

I can identify the key points in the text.

I can use synonyms to rewrite some of the key points.

Excellent progress »»»

I can identify and categorise the key points in the text.

I can paraphrase the text using synonyms and concision.

Summarise effectively using complex sentences

You will learn how to

- synthesise ideas using complex sentences.

Once you have made notes on key points from a text, grouping them into complex sentences can help you express those ideas concisely.

Getting you thinking

Read this account of a bus journey in northern India. The writer has realised that his journey may be more dangerous than he'd imagined.

Once I was actually en route to Kaza, however, I immediately realized that my whimsical pilgrimage could get me killed. The copy of the *Hindustan Times* that I'd bought in Shimla, for instance, devoted an entire front-page story to grisly mountain bus crashes. 'At least 40 people were killed when a bus plunged into a tributary of the Ravi River yesterday evening,' the article read. 'Earlier in the day, eight people died and thirteen were injured when a truck carrying them fell into a gorge 35 kilometres from Manali.'

The Indian highway signs were not much more encouraging. In lieu of shoulders or guardrails, dangerous curves on the mountain featured boulders with white-painted slogans that read 'O God help us!' or 'Be safe! Use your horn'. I kept staring out at the river valley 300 metres below and imagining our driver cheerily honking the horn as we all plummeted to certain death.

The most alarming part of the Himalayan bus ride, however, was the road itself, which seemed to be buried under massive mudslides at 30-kilometre intervals. Indeed, every couple of hours, our bus driver would screech to a halt and I'd peer out of the window to see what had formerly been the road lying in a crumpled crust 20 metres down the mountain. Invariably, several dozen Indian highway workers would be making a frenzied effort to carve a makeshift dirt track into the flank of the mud wall in front of us.

Rolf Potts, *Marco Polo Didn't Go There*

1 Use a table like the one below to list key phrases in the passage that relate to the author's concerns about the Himalayan roads. Then adapt them into a shorter note form, as shown.

Original	Note form
'I immediately realized that my whimsical pilgrimage could get me killed.'	Dream could end in disaster
'The *Hindustan Times* that I'd bought in Shimla, for instance, devoted an entire front-page story to grisly mountain bus crashes.'	

Exploring the skills

When turning these notes into summary sentences, you can use *compound* or *complex* sentences to group ideas together. The example below shows how a student has combined the point about Potts's initial dreams with the news articles and the lack of road protection.

> Having dreamt of this journey, Potts is shocked by the reports of fatal accidents and by the lack of safety barriers on the road.

— subordinate clause

— main clause

This allows the ideas to flow and link together.

2 How has the student used his own words here to paraphrase what is in the passage?

Developing the skills

3 Below are four points made in response to a slightly different summary task – the problems with the roads and the bus company's attempts to cope with them.

Handwritten warnings on boulders.

Roads often covered by fallen mud.

Roads collapsing down side of mountain.

Temporary road has to be made on the spot.

Turn two or three of these points into one complex sentence. Begin:

> Although the journey is halted by fallen mud…

Applying the skills

4 Now, write a longer summary of no more than 150 words about the problems of the roads and how the bus company deals with them.

Checklist for success

✔ Use your own words where possible.

✔ Synthesise several points or ideas into complex sentences.

Check your progress:

Sound progress 》》

I can write a simple summary of the problems on the roads.

Excellent progress 》》》

I can refer to the whole text when summarising the problems and how they are dealt with.

Check your progress

Good progress ⟫

☐ I can select key ideas from a text and rewrite them using some synonyms.

☐ I can identify the relevant points in a passage and turn them into simple notes and sentences.

Excellent progress ⟫⟫

☐ I can paraphrase the text using a range of strategies including using synonyms and concision.

☐ I can find relevant points, turn them into notes and then synthesise them in complex sentences.

What's it all about?

Writing to narrate and describe means engaging your reader through vivid settings, distinctive characters and compelling storylines. To write successfully, you will need a wide vocabulary and the ability to adapt and vary sentence and paragraph structures to keep your reader 'hooked'.

This chapter will show you how to

- improve and build vocabulary to create characters and settings
- use tenses to sequence events and create drama
- use a range of sentence structures for different effects
- use dialogue to advance plot and improve characterisation
- use commas and semicolons to add descriptive detail
- use paragraph structures to position the reader
- structure stories creatively to interest the reader
- structure description creatively.

You will write

- a monologue on the theme of imprisonment
- a first-person narrative about being lost in a hostile environment
- the opening to a story that deals with the 'madness' of the main character
- the opening to a story that involves an encounter at a train station
- a personal description of someone you know well who is a good listener
- a short story on the theme of natural disasters
- the first draft of a story based on the theme of revenge
- a descriptive account called 'City Streets' or 'Early Morning Market'.

Improve and build vocabulary to create characters and settings

You will learn how to

- distinguish between concrete and abstract nouns and ideas and use these effectively
- use nouns, noun phrases and adjectival phrases to create vivid characters and settings.

Storytelling and description both require you to create memorable settings and characters with distinctive traits. To do this, you need to be able to appeal to the reader's senses through well-chosen vocabulary.

Getting you thinking

Read this description.

> The situation was hopeless; I felt fear, loneliness and isolation. There seemed to be no prospect of escape.

 Can you picture this speaker? What has happened to her? What do you see?

Take two or three minutes to think, and then write a description of this person and her story. Simply put down what you imagine.

Now read an alternative version of the same story.

> The rough, steel door in the depths of the heaving ship slammed shut behind me, and the harsh voices of my captors receded into the distance. By now my skin should have been tanned, but as I stared at my reflection in the broken and dusty mirror hanging from the wall, under my eyes I noted the grey bags and the streaks left by my tears. It seemed a long, long time since, as newlyweds, Steve and I had set out on our beautiful, shining yacht to sail around the world.

2 Write brief answers to these questions.

  a) What do you think has happened to the narrator?

  b) How do you know? Are you told directly, or is it **implied**?

  c) What background information is revealed about the narrator and her life?

3 Compare the two openings of this story.

  a) What are the main differences between them (apart from their length)?

  b) How easy would it be to draw an image or make a film of the second? Explain your answer.

Glossary

implied: suggested indirectly. For example, writing 'Having no one to talk to as a child was both a blessing and a curse' might imply the narrator was an only child. 'I was an only child' says it directly.

Exploring the skills

Concrete nouns are words for things that can be touched or seen. For example, 'mirror' is a concrete noun. *Abstract nouns* tend to be emotions – qualities such as 'fear'.

4 Which of these nouns are concrete and which are abstract?

>   despair   lake   dagger   attitude   necklace
>   pride   power   fingernail   ladder

Concrete qualities – such as sound, touch, texture, colour, smell and taste – are key to good description. Abstract references – for example, nouns such as 'fear' – have their place, but on their own they are not enough to paint a picture or show what is happening.

5 Sort these concrete nouns, adjectives and verbs into their qualities (some might suggest more than one sense).

>   acrid   splintered   rusty   pungent   smoky
>   rattle   amber   dull   creaking   shrill
>   echoing   fresh   dented   iron   frothy
>   salty   bloody   wrinkled   shredded   misty
>   groan   windswept

Sound	Sight/ colour	Touch/ texture	Smell	Taste

Developing the skills

One key way to create vivid pictures in the reader's mind is to create *noun phrases* by building detail around a basic noun.

The rough, steel door in the depths of the heaving ship...

— determiner
— pre-modifier (adjectives)
— central noun or head
— post-modifier

6 List at least two other noun phrases from the second text that have been constructed in this way. Then write them out and divide them up as shown in the example above.

7 Now have a go at developing noun phrases yourself. Imagine the narrator was able to stare out of a porthole at the sea all around her. Copy and complete this sentence:

I watched the _____ / _____ / sea / _____.

Top tip

Do not *over-modify* nouns, or they will seem exaggerated. For example, 'the rough, steel, worn, shabby and hard door in the dingy, dark depths of the heaving, swaying and rocking old ship' is overkill!

It is equally important to pay attention to the *verbs* you select. The more specific the better. In the text the writer says, 'the door *slammed*'. She could have said 'closed' or simply 'shut', but 'slammed' describes the sound that is made – and also suggests aggression.

8 Copy and complete this later section from the same story, either replacing the highlighted verbs with more specific ones or adding verbs in the spaces.

Seeing a chance for freedom, I _____ over the side of the ship, onto the ladder, but slipped and fell into the icy waters below. I moved around in the water for several minutes and then finally, I got hold of the side of the dinghy and _____ into it. I was safe, at least for a moment. 'Start rowing!' I said and Steve did so.

Adjectival phrases are another way of building vivid detail about a character. For example:

The man was very heavily tattooed.

— adverbs modify 'tattooed'
— adjective

Alternatively, you could turn this into a noun phrase as part of a longer sentence:

A very heavily tattooed man came through the door. ——— noun phrase

Applying the skills

9 Write a monologue based on the theme of 'imprisonment' from the point of view of the prisoner.

Top tip

Words that have the ability to suggest several qualities can be very evocative: for example, 'smoky' might evoke taste, touch, sight and smell. To be really original, you could even use it to evoke a sound.

Checklist for success

✔ Show, don't tell: you can tell the reader how the character feels using abstract ideas ('fear', 'hope'), but it is far better to show their actions, describe their surroundings and evoke or imply their fear through concrete vocabulary choices and images.

✔ Consider how references to the senses can help create a vivid setting or character.

✔ Build detail by expanding noun and verb phrases, by adding pre- and post-modifiers. Try to do this subtly, making the writing flow.

Check your progress:

Sound progress ⟩⟩⟩
I can use concrete nouns and noun phrases in my monologue.

Excellent progress ⟩⟩⟩
I can use concrete nouns and noun phrases, and use a wide vocabulary related to the senses to create an atmospheric monologue.

Use tenses to sequence events and create drama

You will learn how to
- use the past simple, present perfect and past perfect tenses to reveal information
- explore the effect of the present tense on voice and tone.

Using verb tenses creatively to reveal a character's past or present situation can make your short-story narratives both convincing and engaging.

Getting you thinking

Read these three possible opening lines to a story about someone stranded in an isolated environment.

> I look at the sheets of ice for miles around and wonder how I will ever get out of this place.

> I looked at the sheets of ice for miles around and wondered how I would ever get out of this place.

> I had looked at the sheets of ice for miles around and had wondered how I would ever get out of that place.

There are three main tenses here:
- the present simple: 'I *look*'
- the past simple: 'I *looked*'
- the past perfect: 'I *had looked*'.

> **1** Think about the effect and meaning of each tense.
>
> **a)** Which one suggests the writer has escaped and is looking back on events?
>
> **b)** Which one seems to be happening as you read?
>
> **c)** Which one is written in a tense commonly used to tell stories in a straightforward sequence?

Exploring the skills

Tenses allow you to describe *when* things happen(ed) and the *status* of events (whether actions or states of being are still going on or whether they have been completed).

Read the following extract from a diary entry written in the persona of a character from the film *Into the Wild*.

I look out of this old camper van at the spring sky, my breath coming in shorter and shorter bursts. I remember how I crossed the river in winter, while it was frozen, telling myself to return before the thaw. But last month, when I prepared to return to civilisation, I could not; the thaw had come early and I almost drowned when I attempted my transit. Now, I am trapped. I have always trusted myself to deal with life, with fate but…not now. It will not be long before…I cannot bear to write it…

Find examples of the present simple or progressive, past simple and past perfect tenses and put them in a table like the one below. Can you also find the present perfect ('I have looked') and future ('I will/am going to look')?

Tense	Example
Present simple or progressive	'I look out of this old camper van'

Developing the skills

How you use tenses can clarify time order and add to the drama.

I had been lying in the cave for many hours, perhaps even days, when I saw a chink of light.

past perfect progressive

sudden single event

Complete this paragraph adding the past perfect or past simple tenses as necessary.

Val and I _____ in the underground chamber for several weeks, when finally we heard the ice above start to crack. We had just stumbled to our feet when a voice _____. Finally, the search team _____ us, and lowered ropes down.

Applying the skills

4 Write a first-person narrative or monologue in which someone is trapped or lost in an isolated environment.

Checklist for success

✔ Use tenses to provide background information about the character and make the sequence of events clear.

✔ Think about how your choice of tense can create drama or immediacy, and explain past events.

Check your progress:

Sound progress ⟩⟩
I can use tenses accurately to establish character and describe their thoughts.

Excellent progress ⟩⟩⟩
I can vary the tenses in my monologue to make clear the sequence of events and create drama.

Use a range of sentence structures for different effects

You will learn how to

- use sentences of different lengths and types for different effects
- vary your use of the first and third person, and introduce ellipses to engage the reader's response.

Selecting appropriate types of sentences – and knowing where to position them – can help to speed up a narrative, introduce something surprising or develop an idea.

Getting you thinking

Read these two very similar extracts from a story.

> I didn't see them at first in the darkness, which was descending as I set off at a brisk pace from the station towards the lights of the city. Then I noticed that they were following me so I began to increase my pace almost without thinking. Behind me I could hear their steps speed up too, so I increased mine again, beginning to panic, and then began to be aware of something else – that I had been wrong about the road, too, as it led nowhere, and there was just a dead end with no escape.

> I didn't see them at first. The darkness was descending as I set off at a brisk pace from the station towards the lights of the city. Then I noticed that they were following me. I began to increase my pace, almost without thinking. Behind me, I could hear their steps speed up, too, so I increased mine, beginning to panic, and then began to be aware of something else. I had been wrong about the road as it led nowhere. There was just a dead end. No escape.

 1 What differences are there in the use of sentence types and structure?

 2 Which has more tension and drama?

Exploring the skills

In stories and description, short or **minor sentences** can

- state a simple fact or event clearly – perhaps to surprise or to clarify what is happening
- indicate a sudden pause in proceedings or a change of direction (literally or emotionally)
- sum up or add a punchline – either serious or comical.

Glossary

minor sentences: sentences that do not contain a subject and/or a verb, but that still make sense (for example, 'No escape.')

Longer sentences can

- explore reasons or consequences

- provide descriptive or factual detail to fill in what is happening

- create momentum with a series of linked events or actions building up towards a moment of drama or release of emotion.

3 Rewrite this next paragraph from the same story. Create a mix of longer and shorter/minor sentences for dramatic effect. You will need to remove some words, and perhaps add one or two.

> I was trapped and turned around to see them circling me as their hoods cast shadows across their faces in the cold winter light. One of them stepped forward and I instinctively took a pace backwards until my back was pressed against the wall. To my right I saw that the door of a nearby house was slightly ajar so I ran towards it. As I reached it, it slammed shut in my face so I had no option but to face my pursuers again.

You could start: 'I was trapped. I turned around to…'

Developing the skills

The grammatical structure of your sentences is as important as the length in terms of adding information and creating atmosphere. **Non-finite clauses** are a good way of economically adding detail to sentences. For example, you could write:

> I turned round to face them. I realised I was trapped.

But if you wanted to avoid the repetitious use of the subject 'I', you could write:

> Turning round to face them, I realised I was trapped.

non-finite clause that has no subject

comma separates non-finite clause from main clause

main clause containing subject 'I' and verb 'was trapped'

Glossary

non-finite clause:
a subordinate clause that does not contain a finite verb (a verb in the present or past tense), but one in its non-finite form, such as an infinitive ('to go') or a participle ('going'); in non-finite clauses, there is no subject, or else the subject is implied

Non-finite clauses, like subordinate clauses with finite verbs, can have different functions.

Non-finite clause	Example	How it works
Adverbial (to tell us more about the action)	'Putting on his dark glasses, the gang leader stepped towards him.'	The phrase 'Putting on his dark glasses' adds detail to the verb 'stepped' and what the gang leader *does*.
Adjectival (to tell us more about the noun)	'The railway underpass, covered in graffiti, felt unsafe to me.'	The phrase 'covered in graffiti' tells us more about the noun 'railway underpass' and *what it looked like.*
To act like nouns (to describe an event or an ongoing state)	'Waiting at the bus stop was boring, but she had no choice.'	This is a compound sentence with two main clauses. The *act/event of waiting* is the subject of the first clause and acts as a noun.

We can also use prepositional phrases to add more detail:

Under the pale lamplight, the girl waited for the bus.

Here, 'Under the pale lamplight' tells us *where* she waited.

We can modify or build further detail into these clauses by adding adverbs:

Slowly putting on his dark glasses, the gang leader stepped towards me.

Not only are we told what the leader does as he steps forward (puts on glasses), we are also told *how* he does it.

4 Copy and complete these sentences by adding either adverbs, non-finite clauses or prepositional phrases.

a) _____, the gate opened only when I gave it a hard shove.

b) _____ walking up the gravel path, I half expected to see my father come to meet me.

c) _____, he had been dead many years, so there was no chance of that, except in ghost form.

d) _____ the decaying roof, I could see ravens staring down at me. This was home, but not as I wanted it to be.

5 Annotate your text with the types of clause you have used.

You can convey voice or persona in a range of different ways, too.

A The fact is, I killed him. It was wrong, and there are no excuses; it was simple, pure jealousy.

Here, the blunt sentences suggest a logical person who is trying to explain something horrific. But the same content could be presented in quite a different voice.

> **B** Mad? Would you call me mad...? I'm as sane as you are! But then the whole world is mad, isn't it? You don't... you can't understand why I acted as I did. You haven't felt jealousy like mine, have you? Have you?

Write brief answers to these questions.

a) What effect has the writer created with the style of sentences and punctuation in extract B?

b) What effect does the use of 'you' have on the style in B?

c) How is the voice of B different from that of A?

Another way to add interest to your writing is to punctuate your text with **ellipses** to suggest hesitation and create suspense.

> After what seemed an eternity I heard a sound. The door opened...but no one came in.
>
> 'Who's there?' I cried, taking a step forward. 'I have a gun... and I'll...I'll use it!'

Complete these three extracts by adding some final words and using ellipses to create a dramatic pause or suggest hesitation.

a) I opened the tiny box and gasped, 'It's _____

b) He wasn't sure what to do as she hadn't come. Perhaps _____

c) Who was the child in the faded photo? I suppose I'll _____

Applying the skills

8 Write the first three paragraphs of a story that begins with the main character being declared insane as a result of his or her actions. Write in the first person and set the story in any time – modern or historical.

Checklist for success

✔ Vary the length of your sentences for drama and pace and to reveal or withhold information.

✔ Use a wide range of sentence openings to clearly portray the place, atmosphere, characters and their behaviour.

Use dialogue to advance plot and improve characterisation

You will learn how to

- set out direct speech accurately
- use direct speech in ways that add to the impact of the story.

Dialogue can give immediacy to a story and provide key information about characters, plot and themes.

Getting you thinking

This extract, from a story called 'Leaving Home', is set out as **reported speech**.

> Dana sat quietly at the table, cradling a cup of coffee, and told her father that she was leaving to work in another part of the country and that she couldn't spend her whole life with him. He sighed heavily and told her that he understood and he had been wrong to keep her at home so long.

 1 Rewrite this extract so that it is in direct speech rather than reported speech.

 2 Which of the two examples has more emotion and immediacy, the written 'report' of the conversation or your dialogue?

Exploring the skills

Direct speech is written in speech marks and set within sentences that include not just the spoken words, but also the description of *who* is speaking and *how* they speak. Here is a later extract.

> Dana entered the kitchen and dumped her rucksack on the floor.
>
> 'You can't carry that great thing, love,' her father said, picking it up for a moment.
>
> 'I'll be alright,' Dana replied, quietly.
>
> Her father put the rucksack by the door, and sat back down at the table, and for a moment she didn't see that he was crying.
>
> Then, she noticed his shoulders heaving up and down.
>
> 'Dad...are you ok?'
>
> He looked up and wiped the tears from his face.
>
> 'Take no notice of me, lass.'

speech marks around spoken words

punctuation placed before closing speech marks

new line/paragraph for each new speaker

Glossary

reported speech: when dialogue is *not* written out as though the two people were actually talking

3   a) Which spoken line suggests that Dana is going away for some time?

     b) Which informal words do both speakers use to imply their closeness?

     c) Why doesn't the writer use 'he said' or 'she asked' for the final two lines of speech?

     d) What have you learned about both characters from this short dialogue?

Developing the skills

Too much speech and not enough description turn a story into a play. Too little speech can make the narrative seem distant and lack immediacy. The best stories interweave speech and description fluently.

> 'You can't carry that great thing, love,' her father said, picking it up for a moment. **2**

4   Add your own non-finite clause to this further line of dialogue (use a verb + ing). Think about what Dana might do and how you can add to the poignancy of the scene.

1 First line of speech tells us the rucksack is heavy and reveals her father's concerns.

2 Non-finite clause provides extra information.

> Dana sat down opposite her father. She took a brief sip from her coffee.
> 'I'll keep in touch every day,' she said _____

Applying the skills

5   Write the opening few paragraphs to a story that starts with the line, 'Stepping off the train, she wondered if he'd be there...'

Checklist for success

✔ Include at least one significant conversation.

✔ Make sure you punctuate and set out direct speech correctly.

✔ Do not overuse 'said' or mention who is speaking each time.

✔ Use description to fill in details between spoken lines.

Check your progress:

Sound progress ⟩⟩

I can punctuate the speech in my opening paragraphs accurately.

I can use direct speech to tell my reader something about the character.

Excellent progress ⟩⟩⟩

I can mix speech and description in my opening paragraphs.

I can use features such as non-finite clauses to create character and mood.

Use commas and semicolons to add descriptive detail

You will learn how to
- use commas to embed extra information
- use semicolons to juxtapose ideas in description.

Adding details fluently into your sentences through the use of commas and semicolons can capture the essence of a character, a moment or a place.

Getting you thinking

Imagine you have been asked to write about an interesting person that you know.

Compile a list of descriptive details that your readers might want to find out about your character – what they look like, how old they are, and so on.

Exploring the skills

Read this paragraph.

> Our dance teacher Simone, elegant and inspiring, once had a leading role in a West End musical. Yet she never boasts about her past or expresses regrets; it is as if her past were just a preparation for teaching us! Her favourite saying is 'It's your time to shine!'

Look at the first sentence. Write out the main clause (the one that would make sense on its own). Now write out the part of the sentence that has been added *between the commas*. What additional information about Simone does it provide?

Look at the second sentence. How does the punctuation help organise ideas here *and* aid your understanding of the writer's point of view?

Developing the skills

You can use *commas* to insert details of characterisation into simple sentences.

The man, tall and dark, left the building.   — adjectives modify the noun ('man')

The man, a large figure in a black hat, left the building.   — noun phrase

Commas can also insert additional plot information.

The man, whom I had seen at the station the day before, emerged from the building.   — relative clause

4 Copy and complete this paragraph, adding commas to make the **relative clauses** and additional phrases clear.

> The derelict church dark and forbidding stands at the end of our street. The stained-glass windows which were shattered by vandals a year ago point like jagged teeth to the gravestones below.

Semicolons are useful when you want to say something about related, but equally important aspects of someone's character.

> Here are two further characteristics about Simone. Create a sentence with the aspects separated by a semicolon.
>
> **1:** gained a part in *Strictly* as a professional dancer
>
> **2:** turned it down to focus on teaching

You can also use semicolons to separate phrases in a complicated list.

> Simone always gives us these really challenging exercises to do: stretching and flexing muscles; sit-ups and press-ups; dance steps that get faster and faster.

> Copy and complete these further sentences about Simone, putting in a semicolon and adding a short quote/example of something Simone might say, using a contraction.
>
> Despite all the intense practice, Simone is always ready to listen to our problems.
>
> She often reminds us, '_____'.

Applying the skills

7 Write two paragraphs about someone you know well who is a good listener or who has helped you in some way.

Checklist for success

✔ Include sufficient details to make your subject come alive.

✔ Use punctuation to drop in these details so that your writing is fluent and engaging.

Glossary

relative clause: a subordinate clause that is used like an adjective to modify a noun or noun phrase.

Check your progress:

Sound progress ⟫⟫

I can use commas and semicolons to list the characteristics of someone I know.

Excellent progress ⟫⟫⟫

I can use commas to add and list information and semicolons to balance two equal clauses about my chosen person's traits.

Use paragraph structures to position the reader

You will learn how to

- begin and order paragraphs in different ways to engage the reader
- use paragraph styles or a sequence of sentences to control the delivery of information.

The best storytellers are good at 'positioning' their readers – that is, knowing when to reveal information and when to hold it back. The length and structure of your paragraphs can have a profound impact.

Getting you thinking

In this extract from a set task, a student is responding to a poem with a **dystopian** vision.

> I awoke to a changed landscape. The streets were empty, the pavements silent, and no birds sang. Blackened lilac petals fluttered and fell from the sky. There was no dawn. There was no day.
>
> Moving down the hall, I contemplated what had occurred. Like everyone else, I had heard the sirens and the warnings, but I hadn't really believed they would attack. We had had warnings before, but they'd never come to anything.
>
> This was different. This was the end of life.

Glossary

dystopian: describing an imaginary place where life is very bad

1 What do you think has happened?

2 Why do you think the student has divided up the three paragraphs in this way?

Exploring the skills

3 What does the writer allow us to find out in each of these three paragraphs? Copy and complete the following table to investigate the style and purpose of the paragraphs.

Paragraph	Style and structure	What we find out or are told	Effect
1	First-person narrator Mostly short simple or compound sentences Most sentences begin with a subject Some use of ellipsis ('the pavements silent' = the pavements [were] silent) Repeated structures at the end	The narrator ('I') awakes to silence. The outside world is described and there are changes to the natural order.	Vivid and dramatic Raises questions and paints a bleak picture
2			
3			

4 How important is the *order* of the paragraphs? Try rearranging them – for example by putting the last short paragraph first. Make notes as follows:

   a) Does the order work grammatically? (That is, does it make sense or would you need to rewrite some verbs?)

   b) Does your new order work in terms of the *effect*? What has changed, if anything? Is your new order more or less dramatic than before? Do you find out information more or less quickly?

> **Top tip**
>
> Using ellipsis (the omission of words) avoids repetition and can give writing a more poetic feel or flow.

The order of sentences in each paragraph is also key. Here, there is a fairly obvious structure:

> I awoke to a changed landscape. **1** The streets were empty, the pavements silent, and no birds sang. **2** Blackened lilac petals fluttered and fell from the sky. **3** There was no dawn. There was no day. **4**

1 Topic sentence tells us what the focus will be and introduces a character ('I').

2 Specific examples 'flesh out' the simple, forceful opening sentence.

3 An even more specific single observation.

4 Final two sentences sum up the paragraph and add to the idea of destruction.

5 Write out these sentences in a new order of your own choice. What is the effect of the paragraph now? Is anything lost or gained? Are there any sentences you could remove from your new order? What would be lost (or gained) if you did?

Developing the skills

Different paragraph structures can have different effects, and the way you structure a paragraph can reflect its purpose. Read these three paragraphs, which all use slightly different structures.

I needed to think. If my world really had been affected by the attack of our enemy, as had been threatened, then why was it that I could still breathe, could still move around the house, and why was it that despite the absence of life or movement, no buildings had been destroyed? I didn't need to think; I needed to act.

I raced down the stairs. I took my phone from my coat pocket and to my surprise the screen lit up as normal. I stopped and started dialling. I would call Jack, if...well, I didn't want to complete that thought.

A faint, strange voice answered. 'Yes?' It wasn't Jack.

---

6 Identify the following features:

a) a sentence that echoes an earlier one in the same paragraph

b) a paragraph mostly using simple and compound sentences with the subject 'I' in an active role

c) a sentence that uses a long 'if' clause to reflect and speculate on what is happening

d) a short paragraph that surprises, and 'sets up' the story to come

e) a sentence that uses an ellipsis to suggest fear or hesitation.

> **Top tip**
>
> You can use questions to create drama and suspense, or to ask the questions the reader is asking: 'What will happen to me?' or 'Should I enter the deserted building?' Such rhetorical questions can be used as paragraphs on their own.

We could sum up the structure of the three paragraphs above as:

reflection – action – problem

The fourth paragraph might focus on:

- solution (we find out who is on the phone and why Jack didn't answer)

- more problems

- more reflection

- action

- a combination of more than one of these.

7 Write the next paragraph. Think about the structure you might need to match the purpose (for example, longer sentences for reflection).

The way paragraphs begin and end is also useful in signalling new directions or building on what went before.

> Liu stood on the remains of the road above what had been the main tourist beach. Ships lolled like beached whales on their sides, cars had been flipped over and flattened like pancakes. A solitary cormorant stared down from a crooked streetlight. This was a biblical apocalypse.

From this point, the writer can make a number of choices: Do I stay with my character 'Liu'? If so, do I

- tell the reader more about his life and appearance
- move him to a new place
- reveal more about his thoughts or feelings
- take him back or forward in time?

OR...

Do I introduce someone new, somewhere new, or a new time or tense? If so, is it

- another scene from the same devastation
- an earlier contrasting scene
- someone who enters the same scene?

Where would your next paragraph take the reader? Try out one of these opening sentences and complete the next paragraph. Remember to maintain a tense and voice (first or third person).

> Meanwhile, sitting in her gleaming office in uptown Tokyo, Kimiko stared at the flat screen on her desk...

> Looking down onto the beach, Liu noticed...

> Liu remembered being here just one week earlier...

Applying the skills

An eco-website is running a short-story competition called 'Natural Disaster'. The winner will get to spend two weeks visiting the Amazon rainforest. Write a story on this theme.

Checklist for success

✔ Think carefully about the purpose of each paragraph.

✔ Match your paragraph's sentence style and order to the purpose.

✔ Consider how you will position the reader in terms of what you let them know and what you don't.

Check your progress:

Sound progress ≫

I can write a short story with paragraphs of different lengths.

I can sequence my sentences for effect.

Excellent progress ⫸

I can order my paragraphs and vary their length to create different effects.

I can suit my sentence style to the purpose of my paragraph.

Structure stories creatively to interest the reader

You will learn how to

- vary story structure for different effects.

The best story writers make conscious decisions about the order in which they structure or organise the events in their narratives.

Getting you thinking

Read this paragraph from a story based on ideas a student has taken from Shakespeare's *Macbeth*.

> He slowly drew the blinds. He would never be free of what he'd done, of that terrible act of betrayal that had shaped his life.

Do you think this is the first paragraph, the very last paragraph or a paragraph from the middle of the story? Why? What clues are there?

Exploring the skills

Most readers expect stories to follow a natural order:

Introduction or *exposition*	May introduce the main character or situation
Development or *complication*	A change or occurrence that upsets 'normality'
Dramatic *climax*	May see the character dealing with the problem or problems
Conclusion or *resolution*	The outcome of the main dramatic event – for good or bad

Having a sense of this overarching plan when you write is very useful, even if you decide not to follow it precisely.

Below is the start of a plan for a story about revenge. Spend five or ten minutes planning the rest of this story. Write 15–30 words for each stage in your plan.

> *Introduction/exposition:* A successful business woman in a hi-tech company likes her job but wonders why she didn't get a recent promotion.

Developing the skills

A range of structural devices can help make your story original.

3 Look at each of the possibilities in the following table and then, for each one, explain how you might use them in your 'revenge' story.

Device	Example	Language feature
Flashback	'It had been five years ago that his sister had disappeared. He remembered it vividly…'	Use of past perfect tense ('had')
Multiple narration (1) or plot lines (2)	(1) 'I saw her turn that corner and never return…' (brother) 'I vowed never to look back at Joe as I left' (sister) (2) '*Whilst* Joe was reading the letter, Suzy was…'	Could use first person for both voices; or first and third person Move from 2–3 paragraphs for one character to 2–3 for next character using connectives or separating lines/stars/dots
Framing device	'The letter lay on the mat. He picked it up and tore it open: "Dear Joe, you may wonder why I ran away all those years ago…well, I have some news for you…"'	Move from third-person to first-person voice Change from past to present tense
Linked start and end	End with the letter mentioned in the opening. 'I tore my sister's letter into tiny pieces and let them drift into the flames. It was over.'	Echoing vocabulary or style from other parts of narrative
Ending with a 'twist'	'However, I'd known all along – for it was I who had told my father her secret…'	Past perfect tense Use of connective such as 'However'

Applying the skills

4   Write a draft of your story on the theme of revenge, using the table below to help in your planning.

Stage of story	Effect required	Language feature to be used
Opening: paragraphs 1–2		
Paragraphs 3–4		
Paragraphs 5–6		
Paragraph 7		
Ending paragraph 8		

Check your progress:

Sound progress 》》》

I have a clear plan of the overall four-part story structure and can use it in my draft.

Excellent progress 》》》

I can adapt my structure and ideas to make them more original by using introduction, development, climax and conclusion.

Structure description creatively

You will learn how to

- vary the structure of your descriptive writing for different effects.

Good descriptive writing is about creating a vivid picture through the specific choice of words. It is also about how and in what order you reveal that picture in your text.

Getting you thinking

Imagine *The Big Issue* magazine is running a competition to produce a descriptive writing piece on the theme 'City Streets'. Two students have planned their pieces, but have taken different approaches.

> **Student A:** I'm going to describe the same city street over the course of about 12 hours in autumn, so I'll begin at daybreak, and follow the description through until the sun sets.

> **Student B:** I'm going to focus on one city street but I'm going to select one time of day – lunch time – and move from one place or group of people to another place or group.

1 What are the differences between these approaches? What other ways can you think of to structure a descriptive piece on the subject of 'City Streets'?

2 Select one of these approaches and note down how you would organise your description in paragraphs. Think about whether there is a 'natural' way to do it. For example, would it be best for Student A to write one or two paragraphs on daybreak, then another couple on lunchtime?

Exploring the skills

When you are writing descriptions, you can think of yourself as being behind a video camera.

The long street lined with shops shuttered and shut slowly awakes. At one end, a café's lights flicker and illuminate, while at the other blinds lift up on a fashion display. Here, a young girl stands outside and stares at the mannequins, then retreats inside and steps into the glass box. Like a ballerina, on tiptoes, she reaches and adjusts an amber scarf on a pale and static neck. On the pavement, a sparrow picks at crumbs in the gutter.

wide-angle shot taking in the whole scene

wide-panning from one side to the other

long shot frames one person

tracking shot follows girl

zooming in

cut to new shot

3 Using a similar sequence, write a paragraph describing a street market opening in the morning. Don't worry if you can't get all the techniques in, but try to consider carefully where you are 'pointing' the reader.

Developing the skills

Paragraphs can also help you structure a description by focusing on different aspects of a scene in turn. For example:

- Paragraphs 1–2: sounds: recycling lorry, sparrows on rooftops, rumble of tram

- Paragraphs 3–4: smells: coffee brewing in café, exhaust fumes.

Or you could write paragraphs from different perspectives. For example:

- Paragraphs 1–2: street-cleaner's view of things

- Paragraphs 3–4: young office worker on their way to work.

4 Take either of these approaches and plan each paragraph for a description of between six and eight paragraphs.

Applying the skills

5 Bearing in mind the different structures that are possible, plan and write a descriptive piece, titled 'City Streets' or 'Early Morning Market'.

Checklist for success

- ✔ Consider a range of devices: zooming in on details or panning or cutting from one place to another; having a different theme or idea for sections of your text; swapping perspectives.

- ✔ Decide whether you will arrange your description chronologically over a period of time or whether you will select one time and explore different aspects of that moment.

Top tip

Plan how you will link the different sections in your description. You could do this through connectives of contrast or comparison, for example: 'However, on the outer edge of the market, trade is slow...'

Check your progress:

Sound progress 》》

I can plan the structure of my description, allocating different ideas to each paragraph, and including a variety of perspectives.

Excellent progress 》》》

I can consider a range of structures for my paragraphs and plan my descriptions to create unusual or original angles on a setting or person.

6 .8

Check your progress

Sound progress »»

- [ ] I can distinguish between concrete and abstract nouns and ideas.
- [ ] I can use concrete nouns and noun phrases to show rather than tell what is happening.
- [ ] I can use tenses accurately to make actions and events clear.
- [ ] I can use a range of sentence types and lengths to make narratives more interesting.
- [ ] I can punctuate and set out direct speech correctly, and use dialogue for straightforward characterisation.
- [ ] I can use commas and semicolons correctly to add and list separate information.
- [ ] I can structure stories with a variety of paragraph lengths for effect.
- [ ] I can order the sentences in paragraphs for effect.
- [ ] I can plan a clear story structure and follow it in a first draft.
- [ ] I can plan the structure of a description, allocating different ideas to each paragraph, and offering a variety of perspectives.

Excellent progress »»»

- [ ] I can use concrete nouns and ideas effectively.
- [ ] I can use nouns and noun phrases, and draw on ambitious vocabulary related to the senses to write vividly.
- [ ] I can use tenses accurately and creatively for dramatic tension, action and reflection.
- [ ] I can use different sentence lengths and types to reflect the voice/persona adopted, and to create tension, drama or humour.
- [ ] I can mix speech and description confidently and punctuate my speech accurately.
- [ ] I can use features such as non-finite clauses to advance plot and characterisation.
- [ ] I can use commas and semicolons correctly to add and list information.
- [ ] I can structure the length and order of my paragraphs for creative impact and effect.
- [ ] I can match the style of the clauses and sentences within each paragraph to the purpose.
- [ ] I can adapt my structure and ideas to make them more original by using one or more plot devices.
- [ ] I can consider a range of paragraph structures for my paragraphs and plan descriptions accordingly to create unusual or original perspectives.

Chapter 7

Spelling and proofreading

What's it all about?

This chapter explains some common errors and how to avoid them. It also shows you how to check your work – and to improve on it.

This chapter will show you how to

- use spelling strategies
- use prefixes and suffixes
- avoid common spelling errors
- proofread your work.

Use spelling strategies

You will learn how to

- develop strategies to help you remember difficult or problem spellings.

Even the best spellers sometimes need strategies to help them remember particular words.

Getting you thinking

Below are two word banks that you might find useful in your English language and literature work.

clarity, purpose, audience, reader, paragraph, sentence, argument, informative, viewpoint, structure, present, organisation, grammar, informal, article, report, factual, bias, opinion, cohesion, convey

protagonist, character, theatrical, dramatic, dramatise, inference, implication, theme, narrate, synonym, parallel, villainous, imagery, unsympathetically, resolution, metaphor, rhythm, prose, relationship, location, atmosphere, stanza, chapter

1 Look at the words in each bank for a moment. Ask a partner to say the words aloud to you while you write them down. Swap over, and do the same for your partner.

Take three or four of the more difficult words (perhaps ones you spelled incorrectly) and come up with one strategy for learning how to spell that word.

Exploring the skills

One common way to remember a spelling is to use a process known as 'look, cover, say, write, check':

- look at a word you misspell frequently
- cover it with your hand or a book
- say it out loud
- write it down
- check your version against the correct spelling.

Choose a word you got wrong in Activity 1 (or another word you often misspell) and try the 'LCSWC' process on it.

Another common way to remember a spelling is to come up with a *mnemonic*. For example, you could remember the spelling for 'necessary' as

- a *sentence*: Never eat cheese – eat salmon sandwiches and remain young!
- a *phrase*: One collar ('c'), two sleeves (2 x 's').

> **Top tip**
>
> Keep a list of words that you often misspell and come back to them again and again. Practise writing them out correctly or trying out your mnemonic several times.

Choose two or three of the more difficult words from the word banks, and come up with a mnemonic to remember each one.

Developing the skills

There are other strategies for learning or remembering spellings, too.

Syllabification is dividing a word into its syllables:

prejudice – pre-ju-dice.

 Write down at least two three-syllable words from the word banks that you can divide in this way.

You can also link words together according to grammatical type – for example, verbs: suggest, imply.

 Copy and complete the grid with words from the word bank.

Nouns	Adjectives	Adverbs	Verbs
chapter	villainous		

You could look for words within words (even if they are not related to the meaning), as a way of remembering: paragraph.

Write down three words from the word banks that have other complete words inside them (not at the front or end).

Applying the skills

Read this opening to a student's exam response.

> Our day trip to France was incredibley boring! It was impossible to go on deck on the ferry because of the atroshious whether conditions, so we were stuck with our teacher for the hole journey. We were told there would be sereous consequences if we went on deck. The waves were smashing against the sides of the ship so I wasn't going outside. I did manage to find an attendent but all he said was that it was especialy bad weather for the time of year and that evryone just had to put up with it.

8 Copy out the text and underline any parts of it that are misspelled. Then rewrite the text correctly.

Check your progress:

Sound progress 〉〉
I can identify some of the spelling mistakes in the exam response.

Excellent progress 〉〉〉
I can both identify and correct the spelling errors in the exam response.

Use prefixes and suffixes

Prefixes and suffixes can be very useful in helping you build and understand the spellings of words.

Getting you thinking

Read the note on the right.

A *prefix* is added to the beginning of words or parts of words to make new words (for example, 'overtake').

1 Write down the four words in this note that have prefixes. Do you know what each prefix means?

> Have left you pizza to reheat in microwave. Use 'automatic' setting for 5 mins. Back at midnight.

Exploring the skills

Prefixes are generally added to the beginning of root words without any changes in spelling.

2 Identify the prefixes in the words below, then write down the meaning of each prefix.

a) review   b) intercity   c) superhuman

d) antifreeze   e) autograph.

substandard = below the level needed

subway = a path/route under a road

The prefix 'sub' means 'under'.

Most 'negative prefixes' can be added without changing the spelling of a word:

- un (which means 'not', 'reverse', 'deprive of' and 'release from')
- dis (which means 'not' or 'opposite of')
- mis (which means 'wrong')

3 Write down three words with each of the prefixes above.

The prefixes in-, im-, ir-, and il- can also mean 'not'.

 Add the right prefix to each of these root words:

a) regular   b) legal   c) possible   d) probable.

Developing the skills

Suffixes are added to the end of root words. Often this is to change the form of the word, for example from a noun to an adjective or a verb to a noun:

- 'inform' (verb) becomes 'information' (noun) when the suffix 'ation' is added.
- 'poison' (noun) becomes 'poisonous' (adjective) when the suffix 'ous' is added.

Spelling errors often occur when the root word ends in a vowel – for example, 'sense' becomes 'sensation,' 'taste' becomes 'tasty'. In both cases, the 'e' at the end is dropped.

5 Turn these nouns ending in 'e' into adjectives:

    a) fame   b) grime   c) spice.

6 What is the rule with the adjectives 'humorous', 'glamorous' and 'vigorous', which contain the suffix 'ous'? (Think about the main/root word and how it is usually spelled.)

Words ending with the 'shun' sound can cause spelling problems.

If the root word ends in 't' or 'te', then tion is the ending: 'invention', 'creation'.

ssion is used when the root word ends in '-ss' or '-mit': 'expression', 'emission'.

sion is used when the root word ends in '-d' or '-se': 'intension', 'tension'.

7 Turn the following words into nouns based on the rules above:

    a) act   b) comprehend   c) complete

    d) sect   e) confess   f) admit

    g) hesitate.

Other common suffixes include 'cious', 'tious', 'cial', 'ant' and 'ent'.

8 Write down at least one word for each of these suffixes and say what type of word each is (for example, verb or adjective).

Applying the skills

9 Check over any recent written work you have done. Identify seven or eight words you have used that have prefixes or suffixes and underline them; are they accurately spelled? Do you know – or can you work out – the rule/pattern for each one?

Check your progress:

Sound progress 》》
I can identify and spell correctly some words with prefixes and suffixes with regular patterns.

Excellent progress 》》》
I can identify words in my writing that have a range of regular and irregular prefixes and suffixes.

Avoid common spelling errors

You will learn how to

- look out for common errors you might make when writing.

There are some similar words that it is easy to confuse. Check you understand these before your exams.

Getting you thinking

Read this short message to form tutors about a school trip.

> Pupils cant bring fizzy drinks on the coach. Its youre responsibility to check there following the rules.

1 Identify the spelling errors. What are the correct words?

Exploring the skills

Using apostrophes correctly is one key spelling skill. Apostrophes can be used for

- *contractions*: when you create one word from two, removing one or more letters. For example, 'they're' = 'they are', 'it's' = 'it is', and 'can't' = 'cannot'.

- *possession*: when you use an apostrophe to show that something 'belongs' to or is part of someone or something.

> **Top tip**
>
> You *do not* use the possessive apostrophe for 'its', as in 'The cat drank *its* milk.'

Rule	Example
When the 'owner' is *singular*, the apostrophe goes before the 's'.	'Steve's guitar', 'France's capital city is Paris'
If the owner is plural and *does not* end in 's', add an apostrophe *and* an 's'.	'The children's shoes', 'The women's glasses'
If the owner is *plural* and *ends in* 's', just add the apostrophe after the 's'.	'The parents' cars', 'The girls' bikes'

2 Correct this article.

> Parents are worried about their childrens safety on trips nowadays. In the past, youd just send them off without a care in the world; now, its a major event. Take my two daughters – we had to fill in a huge form for a trip to a local park. We had to note down all the girls medical ailments. Anyone wouldve thought they were going to Timbuctoo! I dont blame the school – its just doing its duty. No, its societys fault.

> **Top tip**
>
> For proper nouns, such as names of people, cities and countries, do add an apostrophe and an 's' if the word ends in 's': for example, 'Jess's mobile'.

Developing the skills

Homophones – words that sound the same or very similar – are a common cause of errors when writing. Here are some of the most common:

- accept is a verb ('I accept the prize'); except is usually a preposition ('Everybody went, except me')

- practise is a verb ('I practise the guitar'); practice is a noun ('I go to football practice')

- affect is a verb ('You can affect what happens'); effect is usually a noun ('the effect of the storm')

- their is a possessive pronoun ('their bags'); they're is a contraction of 'they' and 'are'; there is often an adverb or pronoun referring to place or position ('We went there last year')

- who's is a contraction ('Who's at the door?', short for 'Who is at the door?'); whose is a relative pronoun ('The girl, whose phone I borrowed, lives down our road')

- past is a noun or adjective referring to a previous time ('in the past') or a preposition or adverb signalling place ('he walked past me'); passed is the past tense of the verb 'pass' ('I passed her in the supermarket').

3 In the text opposite, the student has made several errors with homophones or near-homophones. There are some additional ones not in the list above. Find the errors and rewrite the text.

Applying the skills

The English language is also full of words with 'silent' letters:

- 'scheme', pronounced 'skeem' (no 'h')
- 'descent', pronounced 'dissent' (no 'c').

4 Read through this short text and pick out the words that have similar silent 'sounds' in them.

> The performance of *Romeo and Juliet* was wonderful. The Chorus set the scene very powerfully, and each character has his or her own distinctive charms. There were echoes of other plays by Shakespeare in the production, too, such as *Richard III* and this created a fascinating link for the audience.

One of the key affects of global warming is the brake-up of the ice pack at the south pole. Whos fault is it? That isn't clear but a recent expedition their lead by international researchers, found that the width of the ice had shrunk considerably. We can't do anything about the passed but we can effect the future. None of us should except the status quo.

Check your progress

Sound progress

I can spot some errors in my texts.

Excellent progress

I can proofread my text thoroughly and correct any errors.

Proofread your work

If you have five or ten minutes to check through an exam or controlled assessment answer, what should you do?

1   First, read through your work to check that it *makes sense*. Have you missed out any words or phrases? Are your tenses consistent? Does your punctuation help the reader follow what you want to say?

2   Then, read your work line by line and check for

- spelling errors, such as words you often misspell, spellings of names, homophones (weight/wait); capital letters

- punctuation, especially your use of commas; have you used them where it would be more accurate to use a new sentence or a conjunction? Check apostrophes, too.

3   Make corrections. If you need to cross out or add words or phrases, do so neatly and clearly.

- Put a simple straight line through the word or words. Write the replacement word above it, if there is room, or in the margin.

- Use the ^ mark between words to indicate a word or phrase you want to add.

Improving writing to inform and explain

Here is an extract from the following task:

Write about a situation or event at which you felt proud of your achievements or those of someone you know well, explaining what happened and why you felt as you did.

We got to the show and we were shown into this big room, with loads of paintings up on the wall. Pete came up to us and sort of dragged us over to his painting, he didn't want us to look at anyone else's. They were rubbish he said.

— vocabulary – too informal

— sentences – comma used incorrectly

You could see clearly it was our dog from the shape and the eyes. We stood their and looked at the famous painting, which was really good. I am amazed Pete has done it. It was good when he was eventually given second prize, though he thinks he should be the winner!

— spelling error – homophone

— vocabulary – lacks detail

— tense incorrect

— spelling error – irregular adjective

I have always been proud of my brother Pete. My brother's really sociable and humourous, too. Although he has Down's Syndrome he embraces life and makes the most of everything. This is why when he told us about the art show at his school, and his painting of our pet dog we definitely wanted to go.

Examiner's comment

We find out about Pete and why the writer is proud, but the structure is weak and does not follow an obvious order. Vocabulary is lacking in detail and is imprecise.

Now read this higher-level version.

I have always been proud of my brother Pete. He is really sociable and humorous, and although he has Down's Syndrome he embraces life and makes the most of everything. That is why, when he told us about the art show at his school, and his painting of our pet dog, we definitely wanted to go.

topic sentence clearly signals this is the first paragraph

correct spelling ('u' dropped from adjective)

Arriving at the show, we were ushered into an enormous hall, which had a vast array of colourful paintings displayed for everyone's enjoyment. Pete dragged us over to his painting; he didn't want us to look at anyone else's. They were rubbish, he said!

adverbial provides variety of sentence starter

more precise vocabulary describes a range of artwork

compound sentence used accurately with semicolon

We stood there and appraised the famous painting, which was incredibly lifelike. You could see clearly it was our terrier from the wiry shape and the little dark eyes. I was frankly amazed Pete had done it, and his own pleasure in his achievement added to our enjoyment.

It was wonderful, too, when he found out he had been awarded second prize; it was so fantastic seeing him standing up there on the school stage, shaking hands with the mayor, who was giving out the awards. However, as Pete came off stage he looked disgruntled. 'Why didn't I get first prize?' he grumbled as he sat down. One thing is for sure, his Down's Syndrome may hold him back in some respects, but he doesn't lack confidence! It is this that makes me feel so much pride.

Examiner's comment

This response explains clearly why the writer is so proud, and provides a detailed account with vivid vocabulary, structuring paragraphs and events in a clear and logical time order. Tenses are used consistently, even though the writer switches to the present tense to conclude.

Task

1 Read the higher-level answer again.

a) **Structure:** how does the final paragraph link to the previous one *and* link back to the first one? What additional details does the second writer include that the first doesn't?

b) **Paragraphs:** how is the overall structure of this version more effective?

c) **Sentences:** what different types of sentence are used in the final paragraph, and how do they help explain the writer's experiences?

d) **Vocabulary:** how is the language effective in explaining what happened and how the writer felt?

e) **Punctuation:** how has punctuation been used across the whole text to assist the reader's understanding?

Improving writing to argue and persuade

Read this extract from a student's response to the following task:

Write an article for your school/college newspaper persuading readers that spending time in the fresh air is better than staying indoors watching TV, or using laptops and phones.

Getting out in the fresh air is a great thing to do for lots of reasons, like when people say that it blows away the cobwebs which means it sort of cleans out your mind. You can think better. Also, you are exercising – this means you walk or run or whatever. Also you get away from stuff that might be bothering you, e.g. family worries so all these things are real benefits of fresh air.

— clear statement, but would be better as a single sentence

— repetitive use of connective 'also' and imprecise vocabulary

— don't use a shortening such as 'e.g.'; use a conjunction or relative pronoun

— could combine this with first sentence

Staying inside is not good for you. People get sore eyes and even arms (just think of RSI) from staring at computer screens or tvs. Plus it is passive. Some people say it's educational – I don't agree.

— disjointed sentence – could be placed as a counter argument in a clause within a sentence

Just think about how a nice walk or run in the country can make you think about life. You can smell the lovely smells of plants and flowers. You get to see views of the countryside and this makes you aware of your place in the world. You can watch out for animals or insects and see them in their own worlds.

— repetitive beginnings to sentences

— final paragraph is poorly organised; sentences could be swapped around to create a strong ending

Every town comes to an end where it meets the countryside. I know people can say that there isn't that much fresh air in towns that you will suffer from polluted fumes and stuff. It's out there if you know where to look. I say that you just need to keep walking till you get out of the town.

Examiner's comment

The basic ideas are sound, but for the text to be persuasive, the key points need to be put forward strongly and clearly and evidence should develop through detailed sentences. Cohesion needs to be improved so that ideas are easy to follow.

Now read this higher-level version.

Getting out in the fresh air is a great thing to do for a whole host of reasons and provides a wide range of benefits. You can get away from matters that might be bothering you, such as family worries, you can put things in perspective, and you can 'blow away the cobwebs', as people often say. The fact is, getting outside enables

— general statement in form of compound topic sentence sets up benefits to be described

— use of 'such as' to provide example in formal way

you to reflect on life and evaluate things clearly, and who doesn't need more of that?

While some might argue that spending time indoors on laptops or watching television is educational, I strongly disagree. The truth is, these are completely passive activities and whatever you might be learning onscreen is, in any case, offset by potential physical damage (for example, Repetitive Strain Injury), sleep problems, and much more. Getting away from this is of value in itself.

Yet perhaps even more valuable is the fact that you can connect with nature. How often do you get the chance to observe the living world around you or to follow the fascinating little lives of tiny insects or birds? Gazing over rolling hills, or even just strolling in a field that has been recently cut, brings you into contact with nature, and, furthermore, makes you incredibly aware of your place in the world.

Even though people say polluted fumes are all you will experience in towns, I believe that you just need to keep walking. Every town comes to an end where it meets the countryside. That is where fresh air can be found. It's out there if you know where to look.

rhetorical question provides logical end to the paragraph

'fronted' subordinate clause sets up counter-argument to be knocked down

adverb intensifies the adjective for more impact

Examiner's comment

This is a well-argued piece using a range of techniques to persuade the reader, such as rebutting counter-arguments and building evidence in longer, more detailed sentences. The structure is generally very clear, with each paragraph doing its 'job' and individual phrases selected for emotional impact.

Task

2 Read the higher-level answer again.

a) **Structure:** how does the third paragraph link directly with the final sentence of the second?

b) **Sentences:** how does the sentence variety in the third paragraph express different ideas about the outdoor life?

c) **Vocabulary:** how does the writer use noun phrases or adjectives with intensifiers to paint a vivid picture and express his strength of feeling?

d) **Punctuation:** in what way are brackets used in the answer to support the writer's argument?

Improving writing to analyse, explore and comment

Read this extract from a student's response to the following task:

Re-read the poem 'Anger Lay by Me' on page 76. How does the poet convey an idea of anger through this poem? Write an analysis explaining how language is used in the poem to create an impression of anger.

One way that anger is conveyed in this poem is by personification, as she presents anger as if it is a person. We can see this where she has wrote 'Anger lay by me all night long', which shows how anger won't leave her alone. Its like anger is a person who is there all the time, so she can't get away.

vocabulary – too informal

tense agreement – incorrect verb form

punctuation – it's/its confusion

Its not her fault she's angry as anger is this person who is always there telling her 'honest words'. Showing that the things anger is telling her are true. Presenting anger as a person makes it clear that she is not responsible for her anger, like anger itself is someone who goes on at her until she gives in.

sentences – no main verb, so not a full sentence

vocabulary – too informal

Some of the words used seem angry because they suggest violence. For example, anger 'struck from my hand the book, the pen', which seems a strong and angry gesture.

paragraph – weak phrasing, undeveloped point

Examiner's comment

The key ideas here are perfectly acceptable, but a more formal register is needed and there are some errors in basic language. The overall effect is quite superficial, suggesting a lack of detailed analysis. Greater development of the points would improve this considerably.

Now read this higher-level version.

The first obvious way that anger is conveyed is through personification. This runs throughout the poem, with anger presented as if it were a man. For example, the opening line, 'Anger lay by me all night long', introduces the idea of anger as a man who is there all the time, so she can't get away.

this sentence outlines the paragraph's topic clearly

complex sentence provides evidence of the paragraph's main point of personification and introduces a more specific idea to be developed in the next paragraph

Anger's constant presence is emphasised by the repetition of the phrase 'all night' twice in the first stanza. This contributes to a presentation of anger as persistent, and we see this further in 'all through the day'. Because of anger's persistence and refusal to leave, the persona appears to feel powerless against him, as shown by her questioning herself in the final stanza with the repetition of 'And can I...?'

> constant references to the presentation of anger provide a clear focus on the question

This sense of anger as persistent and the persona as weakened by him also helps to create an impression of her anger as something that is not her fault. It almost seems as if anger is something that imposes itself on her, rather than an emotion that comes from her. This sense of the persona's anger as being outside her control is also supported by the phrase 'his honest words' in the final stanza. This phrase clearly presents anger as telling the truth, suggesting that the persona is right to be angry.

Anger is also conveyed as a violent emotion/character through the use of the strong verb 'struck'. The unusual sentence structure here of 'struck from my hand the book' focuses our attention on the violent action against her hand, highlighting anger's physical effect on her.

Examiner's comment

This analysis is sound, using language effectively to present a discussion of the poem. The structure of the analysis clearly shows the student's thinking and demonstrates progression in his or her points.

Task

3   Read the higher-level answer again.

   a) **Structure:** how does the third paragraph link with the second?

   b) **Paragraphs:** how do the paragraph structures in the third and fourth paragraphs help the student to analyse effectively?

   c) **Sentences:** how do some of the subordinate clauses in the third paragraph help the student to provide more detailed analysis?

   d) **Vocabulary:** how does the writer use varied verbs to analyse and answer the question?

Improving writing to summarise

Read this student's response to the following task:

Read the extract about falconry on pages 41–42. Then, in your own words, summarise the appeal of falconry and how the sport links to the past. Write a maximum of 150 words.

This summer, there will be lots of outdoor events and fairs. A falcon (a type of hawk) will be let loose and then return to its trainer following a series of commands and actions.

> this paragraph is not strictly about the appeal of falconry

This is a dramatic spectacle that everyone will love. They will be entranced as they watch the falcons swoop down from trees or from high up.

> this paragraph contains the right sort of information but it is too similar to the original

Then the training starts, which is when the falconer makes the falcon do what he likes. This is highly skilled and it begins with 'manning'. Then the training can begin. This uses a line called a 'creance'. The falcon comes a short distance to start with and then you can increase the distance. After a while you can let the bird fly freely.

> most of this paragraph is irrelevant; the information needs to be tied into the appeal of falconry

Shakespeare used words about falconry in one of his plays. This is an important thing to remember too.

> this paragraph needs to be expanded and linked to the point about the history of falconry

Examiner's comment

This summary is largely lifted directly from the original text. The writer needs to select the appropriate and relevant information, note it down and then construct paragraphs that explain the two key areas mentioned in the task. Paraphrasing of key information in the student's own words is also required.

Now look at this higher-level response to the task. The student has made notes first under two headings in order to *plan* the answer. Making notes like this is a key element of summarising texts.

Appeal of falconry

- 'Dramatic spectacle' – skills are full of action
- 'Entrance spectators' – everyone 'glued' to the spectacle
- 'Highly skilled' – lots of elements that deserve admiration
- Used for 'exhibitions and even weddings'

Links to the past

- 'Hunting animals in their natural habitat' – how hunters used to hunt
- 'Specialised words' – words still used today
- Shakespeare, 'Taming of the Shrew' – evidence

The student then uses the notes to write a two-paragraph summary.

Falconry is very appealing as it provides an exciting sight as the trainer puts his or her hawk through its paces. People enjoy seeing the hawks plunge gracefully from great heights in response to their trainer's commands. They also admire the techniques the trainer uses to control the actions of the birds. It has become so popular that people even hire falconers to attend weddings or other formal occasions.

Falconry is linked to the past through the fact that it is an ancient sport practised by hunters. The terms used all those years ago still survive today. In fact, Shakespeare's play 'The Taming of the Shrew', which is over four hundred years' old, contains action in which the main protagonist refers to hawks when talking about his wife. This demonstrates its strong link to prior ages, but also how falconry has developed over the years to become a mainly leisure-driven pursuit.

— paraphrase of 'dramatic spectacle'

— information from end of original text combined with information from start

Examiner's comment

Relevant points are selected and noted clearly for the next stage of the process. In the summary itself, the writer draws on these points and concisely brings together key ideas and information, paraphrasing skilfully and appropriately.

Task

4 Read the higher-level answer again.

a) What element of the original text is dealt with in the second half of the summary?

b) Identify all the examples of paraphrasing in the answer.

Improving writing to narrate and describe

Read the following opening to a story, which is one student's response to the following task:

Write a story that is based on, or inspired by, any factual programme you have seen or listened to about extreme weather.

I felt so frightened when the storm hit us. I could see the black clouds gathering on the horizon in the morning. I didn't think they would get to us but they did. We were ready but not really prepared emotionally.

— is this the best opening sentence? It tells rather than shows the reader what is happening

— the lack of sentence variety does not create tension or drama

The clouds came towards us like an army and invaded our town. The howling wind came as well and surrounded us. We went quickly to the underground shelter and hid. The storm rattled the door of the shelter again and again. But it couldn't get in. The noises outside were awful. We imagined terrible things.

— weak verbs don't really convey the movement of the weather

— accurate sentences, but does the short, clipped style help or hinder?

I realised that our dog, Scruff, was missing. I went quickly to the trap-door for the shelter but my mum wouldn't let me out. She told me it was too dangerous. I told her I was going out whatever and broke free of her. I opened the trap-door and went outside. All I saw was devastation all around. My mother cried at me to get back in, but I began to crawl slowly across the yard. There was dust blowing everywhere and the biggest hailstones you have ever seen. Our house looked ok. We had boarded the windows. But my bicycle was up on the roof. Then I saw a tiny creature, which was Scruff and I felt so glad he was still alive...

— direct speech would add to the immediacy in this section

— this sentence needs further detail

— new paragraph?

> **Examiner's comment**
>
> There are some interesting plot ideas here, but the writer could have held back information, and drama could have been added to the text with use of direct speech and greater sentence variety.

Now read this higher-level version.

I didn't think they would get to us but they did.

I had seen the black clouds gathering on the horizon in the morning but they had seemed distant, like the backdrop of a film-set, and it wasn't until my parents started hurrying around the house, boarding up the windows, tying down anything that could move that it really struck me. The storm was coming.

— short, one-sentence paragraph holds back information through pronoun 'they'

— long second sentence, using the past perfect for a completed action, takes reader back to earlier events

— short final sentence using past continuous (-ing') adds drama

By mid-afternoon we were under siege. The clouds swarmed towards us like a huge, menacing army and invaded our town. The howling wind intensified and surrounded the house, swirling like an invisible dervish under the shutters and through the roof tiles.

We raced to the underground shelter and flung ourselves in. The wind rattled the door and bullets of rain machine-gunned the earth, but neither breached the shelter. We imagined terrible things: our cattle on rooftops, friends caught in their cars as the tornado struck...our dog...Where was our dog? I looked around quickly. Scruff was missing.

I made for the trap-door and began to climb up the wooden steps.

'You stay there!', cried my mother. 'It's far too dangerous outside.' She put a hand on my arm, but I broke free, tearfully.

'I'm getting Scruff,' I said, flinging myself from her and out of the door.

Devastation faced me. Hailstones the size of marbles had shattered our truck window, and the old apple tree in the yard had been ripped from its roots like a rotten limb and now lay twisted and broken on the ground. Scruff was nowhere to be seen.

Examiner's comment

This response features a variety of sentence styles and lengths designed for impact and effect. The thoughtful use of pronouns and determiners withholds information so the reader is engaged from the first sentence, and the vivid descriptions paint a clear and compelling picture. Striking images and sparse, but relevant, dialogue create a convincing overall opening.

Task

5 Look back over the second response.

a) **Structure:** what is the main focus of the third paragraph? Which is the topic sentence and how do the other details provide further specific information?

b) **Sentences:** how does the sentence variety in the remainder of the text add to the narrative impact and help to fill in more detail?

c) **Vocabulary:** how does the writer make descriptions vivid through his/her choice of active verbs?

d) **Punctuation:** in what way does the punctuation add to the drama?

Check your progress

Sound progress ⟫

- I know how to use the 'Look, cover, say, write, check' strategy and basic mnemonics, such as using the letters or syllables in a word to make a phrase.

- I can form words using common prefixes or suffixes with regular patterns.

- I can use apostrophes for contraction and possession accurately, and tell the difference between some common homophones.

- I can check my work for spelling and punctuation errors.

Excellent progress ⟫⟫

- I can select from a wide range of spelling strategies, including ones related to the meaning or structure of the word.

- I can form words using a range of prefixes and suffixes in both regular and irregular patterns.

- I can use apostrophes accurately in all aspects of my writing and do not make errors with homophones.

- I can proofread my work to fix errors and improve the content.

Teacher Guide

To the teacher

The core aim of this book is to teach students how the application of grammatical knowledge can improve their writing across a wide range of key areas in GCSE and IGCSE. The important word here is 'application'. Knowledge about language is all very well for its own sake, but getting your students to see why it matters and how it can improve their writing at word, sentence, paragraph and text level is our goal. More importantly, it is a goal subscribed to by most English teachers, examiners and professional writers. Furthermore, by linking specific grammatical knowledge and language features to the writing purposes common to GCSE and IGCSE assessment, students can see, for example, that developing skills of concision with complex sentences really can improve summary (see Chapter 5), that intensifiers really do make an argument sound convincing and robust (see Chapter 3), and that modal forms are vital when hypothesising in explanatory texts (see Chapter 2) – to name just a small number of the areas addressed by the book.

Each unit is designed as a mini-tutorial. Students begin with a short task ('Getting you thinking'), which allows them to 'dip their toes' in the particular grammatical idea. 'Exploring the skills' introduces them to the core knowledge they will need to make use of the grammatical construct or idea, and try it out in small steps. 'Developing the skills' takes them a stage further, either through practising elements of what they have learned or by introducing a related, slightly more complex skill. Finally, 'Applying the skills' sets a writing task that is close in style or form to a typical GCSE task, and expects them

to apply the whole range of skills they have learned independently. These are stimulating and engaging written tasks, such as an opinion piece on going to music festivals (Chapter 3) or a narrative about someone lost in a hostile environment (Chapter 6), and they will, we hope, inspire the whole range of students whose progress you are responsible for.

Having said all this, it may seem strange that we have chosen to open the text with a 'Basics' section. However, we felt it was vital that the individual units were not overburdened with re-teaching of core concepts or 'naming of parts'. By having this up front, you can choose to use it as an introductory catch-up, or as an ongoing point of reference – or, indeed, both.

The book concludes with a chapter focusing on spelling and proofreading. It includes five sample extracts from GCSE-style responses at different levels, and asks students to identify the specific grammatical features that make the higher response more coherent, cohesive, vivid or engaging.

Answers to all the main activities can be downloaded from the Collins Education website, by following the link from the series homepage: www.collins.co.uk/aimingfor

We hope the book demonstrates that learning about grammar does not need to be dry, even in the pursuit of improved grades and marks, and we hope we have offered purpose, context and content in equal measure.

Mike Gould
Paul Higgins
Beth Kemp

Author Biographies

Mike Gould is a former Head of English and an experienced author who has written over 150 books and other resources for teachers and students, including GCSE and IGCSE textbooks and digital support material. He has also been a Senior Lecturer in English and Education, teaching the history of the English language, creative writing and how to apply new technologies to the English classroom.

Paul Higgins was chair of the National Association of Advisers in English and led a national programme of continuing professional development in teaching grammar.

Beth Kemp is an experienced teacher and examiner of GCSE and A Level English Language, and has contributed to textbooks and teaching resources for key stages 3 to 5 in English.

1 Understand vocabulary

Getting you thinking
This works well as a paired task to help students think aloud. As an extension task, ask them to experiment with swapping around the replaced words to emphasise, for example, that 'gyre' and 'gimble' are both verbs.

Exploring the skills
Students may need some time to digest the grammatical information in this topic and should be encouraged to come back to it as they work through other topics that make reference to word classes.

As students explore the tables on verbs on pages 7–8, it is worth noting that the verbs 'to be', 'to do' and 'to have' are known as *primary verbs*, because they can be used as auxiliary verbs or as main verbs ('I have a dog'; 'I have walked the dog').

Developing the skills
This section focuses on small function words and would be effective as paired work. It could also be used as an extension only, to allow lower-attaining students to focus on the main word classes.

Applying the skills
This section can be completed for homework to consolidate the lesson.

2 Understand clauses and phrases

Getting you thinking
Students can work in pairs or individually for this task. It would be useful to draw together students' responses and ensure all are comfortable with the terms main verbs, auxiliary verbs and tenses before moving on to the new material.

Exploring the skills
Feedback could usefully be drawn from the class following this task, to compare the sentences constructed, before moving on to the next section.

Developing the skills
The activities here on phrases and clauses could be completed collaboratively or independently. In Activity 6, point out the modal verbs 'could' and 'will'.

Applying the skills
This writing task is best completed independently. As an extended task, ask students to write the full letter. Peer-assessment of this task is another way to consolidate understanding of clauses, phrases and agreements.

3 Understand sentence structures

Exploring the skills
Activity 3 may be a good place to make the point that commas cannot join main clauses instead of conjunctions; only semicolons can.

For Activity 4, students may need to make small adjustments – for example, removing a subject to avoid using it twice in a compound sentence.

Developing the skills
Following Activity 7, ask students to swap paragraphs and check that they can identify the simple, compound and complex sentences used.

Applying the skills
Activity 8 can usefully be completed in class as a paired activity, with the subsequent writing in Activity 9 as a follow-up homework.

4 Use punctuation accurately

Getting you thinking
In Activity 1, try getting students to work 'against the clock', with a timer, to identify as many uses of punctuation as they can.

Exploring the skills
Activities 3, 5 and 6 appear much simpler than they are and could take some students quite a long time to complete, as they rely on grammatical understanding to recognise how the sentences are made up.

Students could work in pairs to complete these tasks, and they should be encouraged to check aspects in earlier tutorials. The punctuation table at the start of this section will help, but advise students to look back at the earlier information on clauses, too.

Developing the skills
In Activity 7, remind student that starting with a conjunction ('Although') is a choice to break a rule for a certain effect.

5 Use paragraphs effectively

Getting you thinking
Use this as a quick starter activity, getting students to use mini-whiteboards (or sheets of paper) to indicate 'true' or 'false' – they just write 't' on one face and 'f' on the other, then respond to each suggested reason for a new paragraph in turn.

Developing the skills
Activity 3 works well as an individual task, with students comparing in pairs once completed to see if they inserted paragraphs at the same points. Activities 4 and 5 are best as individual tasks, leading up to individual writing for Activity 6.

Applying the skills
This task can be completed for homework to consolidate learning so far, and could be assessed as a conclusion to the topics in this chapter, with students warned that their grammatical choices overall will be evaluated in this letter.

Chapter 2   Writing to inform and explain

1 Use precise and appropriate vocabulary

Getting you thinking
Students can work in pairs to compare the two texts, with feedback to elicit the informality of the first and the technical language and formality of the second.

Exploring the skills
Students should articulate out loud what the *tone* of a piece means, using terms they have learned such as 'lexicon', 'formal' and 'informal', and 'possessive determiner'.

Developing the skills
Read aloud the text on adverbs and adverbials, and the Leni Riefenstahl extract, then ask students to work individually on Activity 7. The answers are: a) 'as a dancer'; b) 'on the Berlin stage' and c) 'in the 1920s'. Pause here to make sure all students have understood how these adverbials add to the information provided. The full biography can be found at www.history.co.uk/biographies/leni-riefenstahl.

As an extension task, ask how the vocabulary suggests that Leni Riefenstahl, although controversial, is interesting and important. Look for words/phrases such as 'seminal', 'breaking boundaries' and 'innovative'.

Applying the skills

For Activity 9, display the 'Checklist for success' first, and concept-check the terms used. You may wish to model the first few lines of the text, using adverbials: 'Long ago in the early 90s, an incredible gadget first saw the light of day…'

2 Write sentences for clarity, sequence and purpose

Getting you thinking

Students may recognise the opening text as a common lateral-thinking puzzle. If not, they might work out that the victims in this case are goldfish and the murderer is the cat. Explain that to make the information clear, the text in this section uses two simple and two compound sentences.

Exploring the skills

Read aloud and/or display the newspaper article about the jewel heist. The focus of the topic is understanding how the different types of sentence play different roles in the report – both for dramatic effect and to provide information.

The follow-up activities (2–5) can be completed in pairs. Students can join up in fours to share their answers before reporting back. The key issue for Activity 5 is that the adverbial 'From that moment' means that the first sentence must move, as it refers back to the 'disappearance' of the men.

Developing the skills

Complete the table as a class, focusing on how the passive must be used for the 'Mercedes van', as it allows a concise summation of the facts in 'found burnt out'.

Applying the skills

Point out that students can use the notes from the fact file in the *Mona Lisa* report here to construct their sentences, although they may wish to vary the order of some of the paragraphs. (Students may be interested to learn that this is a true event.)

3 Use punctuation, prepositions and prepositional phrases to explain clearly

Getting you thinking

Students work on their own and can then share responses as a whole class. Elicit the fact that the missing words in the first set are those that tell us where things or people are located – these are prepositions or prepositional phrases.

Exploring the skills

They should compare their rewritten messages with a partner and see if the messages now make sense. Did they agree on the punctuation? Did they select the same prepositions?

Developing the skills

Remind students that prepositional phrases act in the same way as prepositions to explain the relationship between objects, people, etc. (add prepositions to noun phrases: *in (prep) + a black dress (noun phrase)*.

Applying the skills

To make this a more creative activity, students could draw a map of an imaginary area for the trail first, or they could base the trail on a real one if one exists locally.

4 Select different tenses and modal forms to hypothesise and give reasons

Getting you thinking
If students have mini-whiteboards, get them to reveal their answers to you by holding them up so you can concept-check who has understood the principle of the clauses here. Make sure they understand which is the sub clause; the main clause is the part that works as a sentence on its own (e.g. 'war will be avoided').

Exploring the skills
Activity 2 could be done as a whole class, with students suggesting positions on the board.

Developing the skills
Activities 3, 4 and 5 could be done individually, then in pairs, and then shared with another pair to concept-check.

Applying the skills
Begin the task as a shared writing exercise, asking students to jointly construct the first sentence or paragraph of the article.

5 Use a range of paragraph styles, including those with topic sentences, to provide information

Getting you thinking
Display the text and ask for comments from the class. Elicit the importance of the adverbs or adverbials such as 'Finally' and 'For a start'.

Exploring the skills
For Activity 3, ask students what additional effect the last sentence has. Not only is it the topic sentence, it also sums up what has gone before – hence the need to lose 'All in all' if it became the first sentence.

Developing the skills
Students can work in small groups reading the text together and then discussing the

tasks. 8b refers to references earlier in the text: the first through the clause 'As has been suggested' and the second through the present tense, 'Don't forget', which refers to the summer displays.

Applying the skills
There is much to include so allow extra time if needed. However, the information is structured in the same way as the falconry text, so students can use this as a 'parallel' text when writing. They should also decide what their main topic sentences will be in advance of writing.

| Chapter 3 | Writing to argue and persuade |

1 Select vocabulary to make your viewpoint clear and influence your reader

Getting you thinking
Ask students to read the dialogue aloud in pairs and then work together to answer the two questions before taking brief feedback.

Exploring the skills
Concept-check the two language structures introduced here – noun phrases and adverbials (here, verbs modified by adverbs)

and then in Activity 3, ask for suggestions to go into the table. Point out that 'simply for the pleasure of the public' is, in fact an adverb modifying a prepositional phrase – 'for the…'.

Developing the skills
Read the two extracts aloud to the whole class, and then ask students to work independently on the three tasks that follow.

Applying the skills
You may wish to begin the first task as a piece of shared writing. You could start with:

'Dear Sir/Madam, It is entirely wrong that…', talking them through how you have intensified the adjective 'wrong' and then asking them to complete the rest of the first paragraph. The final alternative version could be set as a homework or as a follow-up task.

2 Use imperative and modal verbs to convey tone and levels of certainty

Getting you thinking
Read the letter aloud, emphasising its aggressive nature before discussing Activity 1. Point out that while imperatives can be particularly effective in texts such as adverts or instructions, they should be used sparingly. Always consider how appropriate they are for the audience.

Exploring the skills
Read the second text aloud to the class, and draw attention to the annotations. Point out that 'auxiliary' means 'supporting', so the modal verb helps or supports the meaning of the main verb. Ask students to work in pairs on Activities 3 and 4. Take feedback and elicit the idea that a certain outcome helps the argument, which is why the modal verb 'will' is used at the *end* of the letter.

Developing the skills
Briefly take feedback on the task; the first suggests possibility – it is not likely or certain 'he will go'. The second shifts the meaning to the speaker, who thinks he has an obligation (to himself) to go.

Applying the skills
Once students have completed their emails, they should swap or exchange drafts and peer-assess to identify uses of modals and the effects they have created.

3 Use conjunctions and conjunctive adverbs to write coherent arguments

Getting you thinking
It may be worth making the point that both 'and' and 'yet' are coordinating conjunctions – so in both examples, each 'side' of the sentence is equal in status – neither point is more or less important than the other.

Exploring the skills
The examples in the table are a mix of coordinating and subordinating conjunctions (such as 'because'). Students can work in pairs on Activities 2–5, and then feed back to the class. For Activity 7 they should work independently. They can use the 'pro-wind turbine' model they have just read as a template – for example changing 'inspiring structures' to 'dreadful contraptions'.

Developing the skills
The full article on fracking can be found at: www.countrylife.co.uk/countryside/article/530828/Fracking-the-pros-and-cons.html#6f48LmwPBvs7CCfQ.99

Read this extract, and then ask students to work in pairs again to complete the table in Activity 9. Feed back answers and point out that the article deals fluently both with what fracking is and the different arguments for and against, which are cleverly woven together using conjunctions and conjunctive adverbs.

Applying the skills

Make sure students are clear about the task, and go over the Checklist for success carefully before they draft their speech. Students could deliver their speeches in small groups or to the class once completed.

4 Vary word and clause order in sentences to create particular effects

Getting you thinking

You might want to ask which of the three versions the ad executive would be likely to choose. It may depend on where and how the text was to be used – for example, as a heading the last might be the best.

Exploring the skills

The effect of swapping the clauses might be less influential than students think. In fact, the key here is that the main clause is still the main clause – regardless of the order – and it would set up further sentences about the dental problems (i.e. 'Because they are drinking very sugary juice from concentrate, children are suffering from increased dental

problems. These problems include increased build-up of plaque…'.

Developing the skills

For Activity 5, elicit how the second part of the clause also uses different vocabulary: the vague assertion 'many people claim' is trumped by the rational account 'experts have reported', and the reference to a percentage provides evidence.

Applying the skills

Students should work independently to write the leaflet. They should be able to refer to the choices they have made in terms of sentence order.

5 Vary sentence types to persuade readers

Getting you thinking

Try to draw out comments on the repetitive nature of the sentences in terms of length, and possibly the way the participle clause here ('that is happening') lacks impact and immediacy.

Exploring the skills

Display the website and then ask students to work in pairs on Activities 2 and 3 together. Point out that the participle 'fighting' here is useful because it suggests the ongoing nature of the work and is not designed as a call to action (for which an imperative would be better).

Developing the skills

Students could work in pairs or small groups for this task, annotating the extract on a larger sheet of paper and then displaying it for peer- or self-review.

Applying the skills

There is no compulsion to do this, but should students have the ability or desire to do so, they could create a mock web page, not just a sketched version.

6 Select punctuation to convey your opinions appropriately

Getting you thinking
Elicit the idea from students that the email sounds 'shouty' and aggressive – and because it's all one tone, the message is drowned out.

Exploring the skills
Students work in pairs on Activities 2, 3 and 4. Check that they are being precise in their comments about the different usages of punctuation and the effect. After they have written responses to Activities 5 and 6, take feedback. Note that the exclamation mark makes the first sentence sound jokey and informal; the colon separates the general point from the examples that follow.

Developing the skills
Read the text aloud to the class and then put students in small groups to complete the tasks. When filling in the table, they may wish to think first about the overall tone of Kermode's text. This should help them consider the effect of each of the uses of punctuation – e.g. to make us laugh at something else that is ridiculous or exaggerated.

Applying the skills
To help students get the tone of the music article right, shape the first few sentences together. For example, you could mimic Kermode's style: 'Right: let's talk about music festivals and how much I dislike them...'.

7 Structure argument and persuasive texts effectively

Getting you thinking
You might want to add some content to the table provided by using a real topic, such as whether people should have to apply for a licence to keep a dog (or another animal-related issue, to fit with the later tasks in this tutorial).

Exploring the skills
Elicit from students which part of the paragraph is 'for' and which is 'against' horse-racing, and then ask which word acts as the pivot around which the viewpoints change ('However').

Developing the skills
Students might not see immediately how the two given examples in the table are linked, so help them to identify how the connection is between the idea of 'nobility' and respect countered by 'scandal' and, therefore, disrespect for the sport.

Applying the skills
To complete the task set, you may wish to give students a set of connectives that they might find helpful in constructing their paragraphs: 'However', 'On the other hand', 'Despite', 'Nevertheless', 'yet' and 'in contrast'.

Chapter 4	Writing to analyse, explore and comment

1 Choose effective vocabulary for analytical writing

Getting you thinking
This activity is suitable for paired work, or perhaps as a think-pair-share task. Ask students to write down the words/phrases they choose as a list, leaving a couple of lines between each so they can add notes on effect in Activity 2.

Exploring the skills
Gaining feedback from students between Activities 2 and 3 will help them to produce effective sentences in Activity 3.

Developing the skills
Activity 4 works well as an individual task, with students comparing ideas afterwards. Encourage them to add their own ideas here.

Applying the skills
Students could complete this for homework as a follow-up to the lesson, or it could be completed as an exam practice task. Alternatively, more discussion of the text could be carried out in class first, to support students in formulating the content of their answers.

2 Choose sentence structures for clear analysis

Getting you thinking
This could be a paired task or students could compare their responses. You could also then take feedback and ask students to work these initial ideas into complete analytical points.

Exploring the skills
Students could rework the model sentence first to explore the effects of using a different order or different kinds of clauses within the sentence. Alternatively, show students the sentence first and use the annotations to explain and discuss its construction and effects.

Developing the skills
Activity 3 can be a group activity, with each member working to a different model. Students then compare their versions within the group and discuss how each offers a slightly different effect.

Applying the skills
Again, this can be set as homework as a follow-up from the lesson, or it could be completed in class as a mini exam practice question. Students could peer-assess using a standard reading paper mark scheme or using a simple checklist to focus on the skills from the topic.

3 Structure sentences to compare and contrast

Getting you thinking
This task could be completed as paired or individual work, with students making brief notes of the main similarities and differences between the poems.

Exploring the skills
As an extension to Activity 3, ask students to consider the effect of different kinds of comparison, and to note down other words or phrases they could use for the same purpose. Get them to think about how they can phrase their points to emphasise particular angles, using adverbs, comparatives and determiners.

Developing the skills
Students could usefully swap work to share ideas and perhaps peer-assess, commenting on the effectiveness of each other's sentences.

Applying the skills
Students' analysis of these two poems could form an extended homework task or classroom exam practice. Alternatively, students could work in groups to create an essay, each perfecting one point, and then combining them.

4 Quote and explain writers' ideas effectively

Getting you thinking
Create a bank of ideas about the poem for students to refer to as they work through the activities, allowing them to focus more on *how* they are writing their answers than on the content of those answers.

Exploring the skills
Ask students to summarise or otherwise re-present the rules in their books for future reference. This could work particularly well if they can go back through their work and find where they have used quotations, and either correct themselves and/or transfer those examples to a new 'how to quote' page.

Developing the skills
This section works best as individual work, although students could peer-assess after completing Activities 3 and 4. Alternatively, all responses (or a selection) could be collected for students to see a range of ideas. The table in this section could be copied into students' books as a reference for future work.

Applying the skills
This task could be completed as exam practice, perhaps with further discussion of the poem, or it could be set as homework.

5 Comment on writers' choices

Getting you thinking
Students will have a range of ideas about what is interesting/worth commenting on here, which could be elicited in a class discussion.

Exploring the skills
This is a good opportunity to emphasise the importance of planning. Discuss with students how they may have noted down three main ideas from Activity 1:

- The sun causes difficulties for us.
- We seem to want sunny weather.
- We are not prepared for sunny weather in summer.

Help them structure a four-paragraph plan for an answer to the question.

Developing the skills
The focus here is on moving past PEE-type paragraphs by varying the order of items within paragraphs and avoiding clunky 'this is because' structures.

Applying the skills
Having worked on their answer as a whole, students should not find writing up this task too cumbersome. Students could be asked to annotate their work to show where they feel they have demonstrated the skills from the topic.

1 Summarise in your own words

Getting you thinking
Display or read aloud the text and give students two or three minutes to consider the questions, then take brief feedback. Point out – if not mentioned – the change from first to third person.

Exploring the skills
Students can work in pairs for Activity 5. Point out that synonyms won't always have an identical number of words (for example, 'regenerate' is synonymous with 'grow back again'). In fact, prefixes and suffixes can often provide a clue to suitable synonyms – as in 're' ('again') in 'regenerate'.

Developing the skills
Remind students that concision is a useful marker of more sophisticated writing. Non-finite, participle clauses can create

economy and fluency in writing. Go through some other examples of collective nouns with students and remind them how pronouns and determiners can be used to avoid repetition.

Applying the skills

You could supply an opening participle clause to get students started: 'Providing food for cattle and game…'

2 Summarise effectively using complex sentences

Getting you thinking

It is worth reading the text aloud once to the class, and then giving them time to read it to themselves before they attempt Activity 1. Remind them that this has two elements – first to identify the key phrases, then to turn them into shorter notes. To do this, they should think about removing unnecessary articles such as 'the' and using suitable synonyms.

Exploring the skills

The given example is a participle clause ('Having dreamt…') at the start of a complex sentence, which links summative points in the form of noun phrases with 'and'.

Developing the skills

Students could work in pairs to choose the points they want to put into the sentence and then try out their drafts. These could then be shared with the class as a whole.

Applying the skills

Refer students back to the other skills of concision they learned in the previous topic – for example using synonyms and collective or more generic nouns.

Chapter 6   **Writing to narrate and describe**

---

1 Improve and build vocabulary to create characters and settings

Getting you thinking

Students work on their own for Activity 1, then in pairs for Activities 2 and 3. Afterwards, take brief feedback. You could introduce the term 'infer' here.

Exploring the skills

Activities 4 and 5 are straightforward, but draw attention to the idea in 5 that many of the best descriptions convey a range of sensations. 'Misty' can be touch or sight – even smell!

Developing the skills

Display the example of the noun phrase and talk it through with the class. Point out that 'heaving ship' is also a noun phrase. Note the importance, too, of the preposition 'in',

which adds location to the description. Ask students to suggest post-modifiers with different prepositions, such as 'by', 'on', 'alongside', 'above', etc. (for example, 'by the grimy porthole').

Applying the skills

Students write the monologue on their own. You could then ask them to present these as rehearsed readings in front of the class, and comment on particularly strong uses of concrete description. As an extension to this activity, students could write from the point of view of the captor as well.

2 Use tenses to sequence events and create drama

Getting you thinking
It is important to reiterate that tenses are more varied than the basic 'past', 'present' and 'future' students may have been used to, and that manipulating these carefully is essential to more sophisticated and accurate writing.

Exploring the skills
The key thing to draw out of the work on the *Into the Wild* extract is that the tenses are fundamental to understanding his situation: the melting of the river is an act that has already taken place (hence the tense: 'thaw had come early') and its consequences are felt now, in the present.

Developing the skills
You may wish to work on Activity 3 as a class, asking for a number of different suggestions to fill the gaps to make sure students fully understand the construction of 'had + ing'.

Applying the skills
Students work on their own to complete a first draft of this work. You could ask them to underline the different verb tenses and then get them to explain why they have used them.

3 Use a range of sentence structures for different effects

Getting you thinking
It may help to distinguish between the two texts if you read them aloud to the class.

Exploring the skills
Point out that there are no absolute rules about sentence types. Not all short sentences create tension and not all long sentences are full of extra detail; the key is to try out different types to test the effects.

Activity 3 could be done in pairs; students discuss their choices before implementing them. This would work well digitally as they could easily try out various options.

Developing the skills
Once students have looked at the examples of non-finite clauses, test their knowledge by asking them to turn finite clauses into non-finite ones using infinitives and participles. Suggest variations (i.e. 'leaving' and 'having left', 'being able to'):

'I left the building. I bumped into Harriet.'

'She spoke Spanish. She was able to communicate with the locals.'

Applying the skills
Remind students that the techniques they have learned can help establish *voice*.

Once they have completed their writing, pin their work on the classroom walls and ask them to peer-assess, making a note of one example from each person of one of the techniques correctly applied.

4 Use dialogue to advance plot and improve characterisation

Getting you thinking
Point out that when turning reported speech into direct speech, verbs may well change from past forms to present ones (for example, 'she was leaving' becomes 'I am leaving').

Exploring the skills
You may want students to copy the speech example into their own books or files with the annotations as a ready reference for correct speech layout.

Developing the skills

It is worth reiterating that students should not over-use any of the techniques they learn about. Having too many non-finite clauses starting with participles such as 'Picking', 'Standing', etc., can make writing as monotonous as texts with none at all. Remind them that non-finite clauses don't have to use the '-ing' form, but can use other verb forms such as the past participle '-ed' ('If asked, Dana knew she would admit how scared she was.')

Applying the skills

Before students attempt this activity, give them five minutes to plan some ideas around what the character is doing or has done.

5 Use commas and semicolons to add descriptive detail

Getting you thinking

The information generated from this first task can be kept and used when completing the 'Applying the skills' task at the end.

Exploring the skills

Students can complete Activities 2 and 3 independently, and then work in pairs on Activity 4. Once they have finished, share responses with the whole class, ensuring that each student is clear about the role of punctuation in the example.

Developing the skills

Point out that the relative clause example is a 'non-defining' one; that is, it could be written more economically without 'whom' (and without the two commas) as 'The man I had seen at the station the day before emerged from the building.' The key thing, however, is that relative clauses act like adjectives to modify the noun – i.e. tell us more about 'the man' (that he had been seen before).

Applying the skills

Students could use the information compiled in the opening task.

6 Use paragraph structures to position the reader

Getting you thinking

The text is a response to poems such as 'Your attention please' by Peter Porter, and the opening to the novel *Z for Zachariah*. The work that follows is aimed at B to A/ A* students.

Exploring the skills

For Activity 3, go over the first paragraph and the explanations in the table carefully with students. They can work in pairs on the next two paragraphs. Refer them to earlier topics that deal with sentence types and clauses (note the non-finite clause that begins paragraph 2), or prompt them to look at tenses (the use of the past perfect, 'had'), which explain events.

For Activity 4, students work in pairs and then feed back responses.

You may wish to complete Activity 5 as a whole class exercise on the IWB, moving sentences around. Draw out how the last sentence currently operates as a sort of 'summing up'. By placing it as the start of the paragraph it would be more likely to raise questions – 'why'? or 'what has happened?'.

Developing the skills

Pairs can join up to work on the tasks here.

Applying the skills

Before embarking on the 'Natural Disaster' task, go through the 'Checklist' points with students to ensure they plan their story well before they begin writing.

7 Structure stories creatively to interest the reader

Getting you thinking
There is no 'right' answer here, but you could point out that if the story followed a simple/conventional structure, this would be the last paragraph as it seems to be summing up the events. However, it is likely to be more interesting as a first paragraph.

Exploring the skills
Point out to higher-attaining students that this structure is deliberately simplified – there may be several complications and dramatic climaxes in a narrative.

Developing the skills
Spend time working through the table of structural devices. Can students think of any others? Can they think of any stories they have read or films they have seen that explicitly use these devices?

Applying the skills
Students could start by mind-mapping or generating ideas for their revenge story before structuring it. Once they have the bones of their story, they should plan it out in the table and then write a first draft.

8 Structure description creatively

Getting you thinking
Students work on their own for these tasks. Remind them that *The Big Issue* is a magazine sold by homeless people to support themselves.

Exploring the skills
You may wish to demonstrate the film-shots mentioned by showing a short clip from a documentary-style film. For the activity, you could do this as a shared writing piece with the whole class contributing ideas on the board. Or ask students to work in small groups on a large sheet of paper.

Developing the skills
Students should work independently now. Remind them they only need to *plan* their paragraphs, so all they need to do is jot down what or who they will describe in general terms.

Applying the skills
Students can use the plan they have developed, or start afresh with new ideas.

Chapter 7	Spelling and proofreading

1 Use spelling strategies

Getting you thinking
Before they start to think about strategies for learning or remembering the words, check all students are clear what 'strategy' means – a way of achieving something. You may also want to give them an example – perhaps a visual one in which a word is written out according to its structures with the same colour for repeated letters, or underlining a difficult 'bit' of the word.

Exploring the skills
Students can work on the LCSWC method on their own, and then after completing Activity 4, share mnemonics as suggested. You could ask students: what makes a good mnemonic? Do they have them in other subjects to remember key information?

Developing the skills
Point out to students that syllabification is fine, but that they it won't always help them, especially as there are so many silent

or unsounded vowels and consonants in English. Written down, we might expect, 'learned' and 'looked' to be pronounced 'learn – ed' (as in 'head'), but of course they aren't.

2 Use prefixes and suffixes

Getting you thinking
Write or display the text on the board. You could ask for volunteers to come up and underline the prefixes shown, and in the cases of 'auto' and 'micro' which language they originate from (Greek).

Exploring the skills
For Activities 2–4, ask students to try to work out the answers on their own and then join with a partner to check their responses.

Developing the skills
For Activity 6 – the rule for these endings is that for nouns ending in 'our', when they take an 'ous' ending, they drop the 'u' from the root word. Students may be able to

Applying the skills
Read the text aloud to students. The correctly spelled words are: *incredibly, atrocious, weather, whole, serious, attendant, especially, everyone.* You could ask – which of these words might not have been picked up by a spell-checker? Why?

think of some others such as 'clamorous', but should also be aware of the reverse 'false-friend'; for example, 'decorous' might make us think that 'decor' should be 'decour' – it isn't.

Applying the skills
There will be some students whose spelling is almost always accurate. If they cannot find sufficient spelling errors, they can be set the task of listing words from their own work that use identifiable prefixes and suffixes and suggesting what they mean, and whether they come from one of the feeder languages for English such as French, Greek or Latin. For example, 'ment' is a common noun ending we share with the French.

3 Avoid common spelling errors

Getting you thinking
You might want to begin by reminding students just how many marks can be gained – or lost – through poor spelling, punctuation and grammar skills, and therefore how taking care, especially in avoiding common errors, is paramount.

Exploring the skills
Go over the key apostrophe rules and ensure that everyone is clear about the different times when they should and shouldn't be used. Field any questions students might have – don't assume they have understood it first time.

It might be useful to work as a class on the full text on the board. You might wish to conscript weaker students to offer ideas as to how the text should be corrected.

Developing the skills
Ask students how many of them make at least one of the mistakes from the homophones in their writing. Have they tried out any strategies for getting them right? Have they thought of any now? They should try to complete the rewriting of the text themselves.

Applying the skills
Students can complete this final task on their own. Finish the work on spelling by asking students to write down one or two new strategies they are going to use to learn key words they misspell. Encourage them to think about the word's function (is it a noun or a verb, for example?) and use some of the established ways of learning it, as well as any of their own they can think of.

Notes